Universal Design And Aging

Keeping Our Homes Safe, Accessible & Comfortable As We Age In Place

Universal Design And Aging

Keeping Our Homes Safe, Accessible & Comfortable As We Age-In-Place

Steve Hoffacker

AICP, CAASH, CAPS, CGA, CGP, CMP, CSP, MCSP, MIRM

Universal Design And Aging

Keeping Our Homes Safe, Accessible & Comfortable As We Age In Place

Cover photo by Steve Hoffacker.

ALL RIGHTS RESERVED.

ISBN: 978-0-615-89566-6

———

Living independently and effectively in the home that you love and having it grow old gracefully with you is the key to successful aging-in-place. This book shows you how (personally or with the help of one or more remodeling professionals) to create and implement unobtrusive, functional, comfortable, user-friendly, convenient, contemporary, safe, sensible, visitable, accessible, and desirable strategies, concepts, solutions, and treatments with universal design that will help you realize this objective of staying in your home.

———

Other Sales Content
By Steve Hoffacker

To access or learn about books, eBooks, articles, blogs, commentary, and other content by Steve Hoffacker for anyone who sells products or services for a living, use the sites below.

"Hoffacker Associates" Website
http://stevehoffacker.com

Steve Hoffacker's Amazon.com Author Page
http://amazon.com/author/stevehoffacker

"Steve Hoffacker's Home Sales Insights" Blog
http://homesalesinsights.com

"Steve Hoffacker's Sales Quips" Blog
http://salesquips.com

"Steve Hoffacker's Success Quips" Blog
http://successquips.com

Steve Hoffacker and Hoffacker Associates can be found online at Facebook, Active Rain, Pinterest, Linked-In, Plaxo, Twitter, Goggle+, YouTube, Tumblr, and other business, real estate, and social sites.

Table Of Contents

Preface

This text is available in both printed and Kindle eBook editions.

Both versions are similar in content although there are formatting differences between them.

This book is another in my series on universal design — "Common Sense Universal Design" and "Universal Design For Builders" are the others.

They focus on making living spaces as usable and accessible as possible for anyone in the home, regardless of their age or physical ability.

However, the book you are reading now concentrates more on the senior population and those who want to live in a comfortable and safe home that accommodates the normal aging process and the limitations that may stem from that.

As is true in the "Common Sense Universal Design" book, I have prepared the content in this book for both the consumer and the professional — making it a great resource and handbook for homeowners or renters who want to contemplate and understand changes they can make or have done in their own homes, and for the professionals who want to assist seniors in adapting or renovating their homes.

While a typical book has a specific audience in mind that it is appealing to, this one is created to educate consumers about available lifestyle choices for them as they remain in their homes as well as the providers on how they can deliver those options to people who need them.

As a renter (in an apartment building, condo building, or free-standing home) or a homeowner — or even an apartment building owner or manager — I want you to use the material in this book to evaluate your home or apartment as being able to meet your current needs plus your projected needs over the next several years as you desire to remain living comfortably in your home and have it continue to serve you well.

For building owners and managers, evaluate how well your apartments can safely and comfortably serve your older tenants.

Whether you desire to make some of the changes yourself, or you want to have them done, use the information I present in this book to become aware of the types of changes to your living space that you might want to consider. These changes will add to your general comfort and overall safety in your home.

If you aren't comfortable making the changes yourself, you may wish to contact a remodeler, contractor, handyman, occupational therapist, or interior designer to assist you.

If you are a professional that wants to understand the types of changes and improvements that you can offer your clients and customers as they desire to remain in their homes as they grow older, I present sensible modifications that are based on universal design concepts and principles — specifically with aging-in-place in mind.

As I'll talk about in the following text, there are so many opportunities to swap out existing features, fixtures, and devices with something more appropriate in terms of accessibility, comfort, convenience, and safety — or to modify existing spaces to create those opportunities — whether you are doing them for your own home or apartment or you are the professional who is providing this work for your client.

While universal design concepts accommodate all ages, I am specifically interested in those designs that appeal to safe and comfortable living spaces for seniors and those remaining in their homes over time.

It's not that we want to ignore children and younger adults or treat them as unimportant — they just are not the primary focus of this book.

I base my recommendations and suggestions on several years (and counting) of teaching the Certified Aging-in-Place Specialist ("CAPS") designation program through the National Association of Home Builders, the interactions and contributions of the hundreds of attendees at these programs, my independent research and earlier books, and the remodeling I have done on my own homes using such products and solutions.

I have no formal training in architecture or design other than the experience gained in teaching the CAPS program and more than 3 decades of consulting with homebuilders.

Nevertheless, the concepts I discuss in this text have been validated by personal experience in the remodeling of my own homes, focus groups with new home buyers over the years, and the concurrence and input of hundreds of attendees at my programs.

You'll find as you read what I have prepared for you that universal design is an intuitive approach that works as an effective solution and strategy for many living environments — especially as a great way to make our homes continue to serve us well as we age.

In fact, there are few homes anywhere that couldn't benefit from the use and application of these principles — unless they were designed that way to begin with or have already been modified.

This is not a concept that is just for the United States, or for Canada, or even North America. This can be applied to homes anywhere in the world.

While the traditional universal design approach accommodates a tremendous range of ages, heights, and physical abilities, our main focus in this text is how it works especially well for aging and for having our homes continue to serve us effectively.

For specific physical needs that might require more particular design emphasis and solutions, universal design is still an integral part of the overall approach and a great place to begin because it already allows for a range of heights and physical abilities.

While the ideas and strategies presented here are based on technology and solutions currently available, it is entirely likely that new products and solutions or even best practices will become available that meet the definition and spirit of universal design and how it is delivered that should be considered for use as they become known.

Universal design can help you establish safer living environments with virtually invisible changes — by adding new elements or replacing existing features and components with more accessible ones. When completed, the features and concepts shouldn't look much different from what they are replacing.

If people visiting your home don't specifically know what they are looking at and what it has replaced, they will think that it is just a creative part of the design.

The key to successful home modifications using universal design is making improvements that are essentially invisible — ones that do not call attention to themselves.

There are specific design solutions that can be accomplished for wheelchair access, but universal design solutions accommodate those in most cases and don't suggest how or by whom the space is to be used.

This book is not intended to address every single area of the home but will provide many solid ideas and strategies on ways to make nearly anyone's home more accessible, comfortable, attractive, convenient, serviceable, functional, and safe as we age and desire to retain independence in our homes — whether you are doing this for your own home or you are the provider or designer doing this for a client's home.

Universal design is a great concept for both interior and exterior treatments. Done with a focus on serving seniors, it becomes even more powerful.

Universal Design And Aging

Keeping Our Homes Safe, Accessible & Comfortable As We Age In Place

---
1

Why Choose Universal Design For Aging-In-Place?

An Overview Of Universal Design

To understand and appreciate why universal design is such a great and intuitive approach for allowing people to remain in their homes and to have their homes be functional and serviceable for them throughout their lifetimes — regardless of their physical condition or limitations — we have to look at what universal design means and what it is.

Universal design is a concept, treatment, solution or strategy — depending on how and when it is applied to the living space — that results in safe, convenient, comfortable, accessible, friendly, desirable, visitable, marketable, and serviceable living spaces for anyone, but particularly as we age and remain in our homes.

It can be used at any point in the lifetime of someone in a particular home. There is no magical time or event that has to happen first before universal design improvements can or should be done or undertaken.

It doesn't have to wait until someone's mature years; however, universal design has some particularly great applications for seniors.

Nevertheless, universal design works for twenty-something-year olds as well as for sixty- or seventy-something-year olds, and any other age group.

That's why it is labeled "universal." It works for nearly everyone in any situation — even people that might have special mobility, sensory, or cognitive needs or concerns.

A Closer Look At Universal Design

You may have some idea of what universal design is, or it might just be a term that you have heard of.

Let me provide a simple, yet comprehensive, definition of the concept of universal design and why it works so well for people who want their homes to continue serving them well as they grow older.

Essentially, universal design means that anyone living in your home — or visiting you, whether for a couple of hours or for several days — can have equal access to any part of your home, inside and out, and enjoy success in using the various features, fixtures, appliances, and controls in your home without any special compensation or consideration.

This means that your guests or visitors would feel as welcome as you in your home and quite comfortable — if just for a few hours or for an extended stay.

Being able to navigate your home or access switches, doors, drawers, windows, faucets, and other facilities or devices would be comfortable and convenient for them — just as they are for you.

No special physical size, height, coordination, or physical ability would be required. This is the beauty of universal design.

It makes sense and it offers a very practical solution and strategy for increasing the safety, comfort, convenience, and accessibility for everyone, regardless of what type of living space you have.

This is the real deal. There is nothing trendy or faddish about it.

It makes sense and offers safe, practical, comfortable, intuitive, accessible, unobtrusive, and contemporary solutions and styles.

Why Is There Universal Design?

There may be many good reasons or explanations for universal design to be used as a strategy in American and Canadian homes and elsewhere around the world.

It is intuitive. It makes sense. It is attractive. It is relatively simple and easy to do.

All that said, the aging of the population is why universal design is getting so much attention now. Certainly all of us are aging, and we are concerned about staying in our homes and having our homes be relevant for our needs.

While none of us likes to think of ourselves as getting older or "aging," it is a fact of life.

The idea of "aging-in-place" or remaining in your home for as long as you choose and as long as you are able to remain somewhat independent is at the heart of the universal design concept.

There is so much to be said for maintaining one's independence.

At some point in your life, you will find a home that you like, that you are comfortable living in, that generally provides for your needs (or can be adapted to do so), and is in a neighborhood or location that you like.

You might already have found that home and are living in it right now, or you might be searching for it.

When you find it, you'll know it. You'll know that this is your lifetime home — the one you want to stay in for as long as you can.

Universal design elements help us maintain our homes so they are easy to navigate and easy to use the various fixtures, appliances, controls, and other aspects of living comfortably and safely in our homes.

What Qualifies As Universal Design?

Essentially, universal design must appeal to and be usable and accessible to the general population without qualification. That's what makes it universal.

In our case, we are chiefly interested in how they can make life easier and simpler for us as we age and remain in our homes.

With the exception of those individuals that require specific design applications for their particular needs and abilities, universal design generally serves quite well for the normal aging process and for those who have various special access needs.

Using universal design treatments and features does not require any advance knowledge or instruction in how to operate something (such as turning on a faucet or light switch, or opening a door).

In addition, the solutions and fixtures must be so easy and flexible or forgiving to use that a person doesn't have to operate them perfectly or "just-so" in order to make them work effectively.

They must be installed or located so that nearly anyone can reach and use them. As we age and don't necessarily have the physical flexibility of reaching as far or standing as upright as we once did.

Using universal design treatments should require a minimum of effort and not depend on any particular height, hand or arm strength, gripping or grasping ability, or range-of-motion.

When used correctly and appropriately, universal design elements fit seamlessly into the living space and become just part of the home without calling attention to the design or sticking out in anyway as something special or unusual. Being unobtrusive is a major design objective.

Why Universal Design Works

In addition to just fitting into your home without being obvious, universal design features actually enhance the appearance, value, comfort, and safety of your home.

Putting in such items as single-lever faucets, lever door handles, or rocker light switches makes your home safer for you, makes the controls easier to operate, makes it more convenient for you and your visitors or guests, modernizes the look of your home, and adds value to your home since people interested in purchasing your home at a later date would look for and expect to find such features included.

Thus, your home looks more attractive, more inviting (for guests or visitors to come to your home and feel welcome), safer, more convenient, more comfortable, and more contemporary (with up-to-date features).

These features don't need to be updated as we age. That's the great part about installing them now. They are relatively timeless because they work so well.

Just Another Name For "ADA"?

"ADA" or the "Americans With Disabilities Act" dictates what must be addressed and in what manner to make indoor spaces and entrances accessible to everyone — especially people using a wheelchair or other forms of mobility assistance such as a cane or walker.

Universal design solutions, treatments, fixtures, components, features, strategies, and elements are complementary to that ideal in many ways. They just aren't required or labeled as such for residences.

Single family homes, duplexes, triplexes, and quads are exempt from the provisions of ADA although some local building codes could require some compliance. Nevertheless, accessibility is a great idea — especially as we age.

Universal design and ADA are not the same thing, however, designing to comply with ADA requirements may make good sense for general comfort and safety.

Is Universal Design Considered Green?

Just as you may have had heard of universal design before picking up this book and possibly knew something about it, green building is another concept that you might have heard about.

What constitutes a green product or a green project is often subject to interpretation, but the basic concept is sound and relatively straightforward.

It deals with the sustainability and optimum use of products so that they are cost effective to use with little waste product generated.

As you read the following text on universal design, you will see some suggestions, concepts, strategies, and solutions that seem to be consistent with green building and design. That's because green building and universal design have several similarities.

However, they are not the same thing.

Nevertheless, whether you consider yourself to be fan of green building or not, the universal design concepts and strategies that I present in this text will help you create safer, more comfortable, more efficient, more convenient, more sustainable, and more accessible homes that have a greater perceived and actual value than similar homes not utilizing these methods.

Who Benefits From Universal Design?

Essentially everyone can benefit from universal design ideals, strategies, and solutions. That's why it has the name universal attached to it.

Moreover, I want people as they are aging and desiring to remain in the homes they love to be able to incorporate such design considerations into their remodeling or updating plans.

You might be contemplating doing the work yourself, or you might be discussing it with a professional that you will engage to do all or part of it.

If you are that designer, remodeler, handyman, or contractor who is going to be consulted and enlisted to do the renovations, I want you to be prepared with the design changes and solutions that you can offer your clients — those that focus on seniors rather than younger individuals or families, even though universal design treatments still apply across all age segments.

You might also be an occupational therapist, physical therapist, other type of health care professional, electrician, plumber, carpenter, real estate sales professional, home stager, electrical service contractor (ESC), durable medical equipment (DME) specialist, home inspector, architect, HVAC contractor, appliance or plumbing fixture retailer, tile setter, cement mason, flooring contractor, flatwork contractor, or structural engineer who will be consulted and involved in helping to make the homes of your clients safer, more comfortable, more convenient, more contemporary, more accessible, more friendly, and more valuable.

Because universal design is meant to accommodate the widest range of ages and abilities, it is not driven by someone's specific physical ability or medical condition.

Nevertheless, this text focuses on seniors and those desiring to live in their current home for several more years — to offer a safe, convenient, comfortable, and accessible living environment.

In addition, universal design is not limited to just owner occupied residences. Depending on the extent and complexity of the design changes desired, many of the strategies I present in this text are appropriate for renters as well.

Universal Design And Aging

As a homeowner or renter, you are looking for solutions and concepts that will help you be more comfortable in your home. You want to be able to use the fixtures and features that you have — or that you add or replace them with — more conveniently.

You want to be safe in your home — whether you are living by yourself or have others in your home with you.

Some of the design changes that I present and discuss with you in this book — or that you discover on your own — will be easy ones for you to do yourself. Others will require the assistance of a family member, neighbor, or friend. Still others are going to require the services of a professional to accomplish.

People age in different ways, and some have more health concerns and daily living issues than others.

Determine what works for you and your household.

Some people as they age have relatively few health issues. They still bike, hike, ski, golf, play tennis, bowl, swim, and enjoy an active lifestyle.

Climbing stairs, opening doors, and accessing and using other aspects of their home aren't a serious concern for them.

Some have a few aches and pains that they live with that doesn't impede their daily schedule or activities that much. In a sense, they have learned to accommodate what ails them, and they manage.

Others have aging issues such as osteoporosis, arthritis, bursitis, and other joint issues in their hands, feet, ankles, hips, elbows, spine, and shoulders. They may have stiffness in these areas from sports injuries or other causes.

They might have various other issues normally associated with aging, such as vision, hearing, cognitive, or mobility issues (how they get around and move about). Range-of-motion, reaching, standing, sitting, stepping up and down, holding and carrying objects, and other common tasks around the home may not be as easy as they used to be.

Regardless of what issues might be present, or might come along, universal design is a great strategy for helping seniors to live well in their homes. It allows for more access, safety, convenience, comfort, use of your home, and general peace-of-mind than any other decorating or remodeling approach.

2

Universal Design As A Solution

The Universal Design Premise

Whether you are a consumer or a provider, if you accept the premise that universal design really is for all ages and abilities, it sets the stage for what we want to accomplish in your home.

Since universal design will accommodate the reach, hand and arm strength, range-of-motion, coordination, and physical abilities of a child (say a 4-, 5-, or 6-year old) as well as a 90-year old, and someone who is normally ambulatory to someone who typically uses a walker or wheelchair for assistance, it then becomes the preferred design strategy for helping seniors enjoy their homes.

Universal design permits accessibility and use of the various aspects of your home — inside and out— in a safe, friendly, comfortable, and convenient manner without any adaptation or other considerations.

There may be special modifications required to address specific needs in your home, but using the concepts and strategies of universal design will give most people a safer, more comfortable quality of life — regardless of age or physical ability. Moreover, the changes will hardly be noticeable.

Over time, the universal design changes that can be made will be even more beneficial from a safety, convenience, and comfort basis.

While universal design solutions and strategies work for nearly everyone irrespective of their physical age, height, weight, or ability, they are quite effective for seniors (feel free to use your own definition of what constitutes a "senior").

Also, it doesn't matter whether you are standing or seated, with full range-of-motion or some limitations, having unrestricted mobility or some mobility issues, with no stamina or coordination issues or moderate ones, and even with moderate cognitive issues.

The Payoff For Universal Design

Major reasons or benefits for wanting to have universal design strategies and solutions implemented in your home or for those seniors you are working with include *safety, security, comfort, convenience, function* (usefulness), *accessibility, marketability* (resale value), *visitability, sustainability* (durable and cost-effective improvements), and *peace-of-mind*.

Any one of these reasons would be sufficient for creating universal design solutions and strategies for seniors, but most people will benefit from all of them.

Safety is a key objective in remodeling a home or apartment, and universal design elements result in more safety because they provide more lighting, easier opening drawers and doors, more stable footing and standing surfaces (inside and outside), easier to use controls, better hygiene, and other helpful solutions.

They also provide convenience, comfort, and economic benefits (expressed in a variety of ways such as having durable features and fixtures that won't need replacing), but mostly they make your living spaces safer.

This also promotes security, both within your walls and around your property. Not worrying about falling, tripping, or stumbling on unsafe flooring or clutter, being able to access controls and windows, having impact resistant windows, and have proper lighting increases safety, comfort, peace-of-mind, and security.

Security is often represented by peace-of-mind.

By making things in and around the home more accessible and easier to use, generally they also are more convenient to use and more enjoyable — regardless of how tall someone is, whether they are seated or standing, or what their range-of-motion, ability to reach or lift objects, or other limitations or concerns might be.

People can be more comfortable and confident with setting the temperature, using various fixtures and appliances, using water at a pleasant and safe temperature, accessing controls without having to reach for them or stretch to see what the settings are, and generally moving about in the home.

In terms of marketability, universal design changes and improvements can make your home easier to sell or rent later on because it will appeal to a broader section of the population and have more actual value or more perceived value — achieving a higher sales price or rent and fewer days on the market.

Think in terms of modernizing your home or living space, making it more contemporary, using newer technology, and achieving more style — in addition to just making the changes because of the safety, convenience, or comfort benefits.

There is a real economic and aesthetic benefit to making universal design changes. Moreover, because they are intended to be unobtrusive and essentially invisible except as a design feature, these treatments have tremendous visual appeal and will be attractive additions to any home.

The Visitability Benefit

A big reason for incorporating universal design changes into your home is for visitability. Of course your personal safety and general enjoyment of your home top the list for making improvements.

Nevertheless, the idea of visitability is a big — and frequently overlooked or ignored — aspect of remodeling and universal design.

This may be an unfamiliar term for you, but it has to do will the ability — or inability — of anyone to visit your home or apartment comfortably and conveniently.

Whenever you entertain or host a meeting, party, get-together, backyard party or cookout, dinner, reception, or discussion group, you want people to feel welcome in coming to your home without wondering if they will feel comfortable.

You won't always know in advance whether someone can climb steps or negotiate a narrow entryway — when that is the case. Maybe someone invites a friend or relative of theirs who has mobility issues.

Therefore, you want to make your home as "visitable" as possible — capable of being entered and navigated without restrictions or limitations by whomever you invite or comes along with someone else you invited.

Also, as we age, the chances increase that our friends and relatives will need some type of mobility assistance (cane, walker, or wheelchair), that they might have balance issues, or that they will have difficulty with hip or knee joints that hinder climbing steps. We may not know of this until they actually arrive to see us.

By making visitable improvement to your home to allow comfortable access to the main public areas of your home (entry, foyer, hallway, living room, dining room, family room, bathroom, kitchen), this shows a thoughtfulness and anticipation on your part that your guests and relatives will greatly appreciate — and notice — when they come to your home.

Where Universal Design Works

To achieve greater safety inside and around your home, to offer more comfort and convenience to you and the people who live in your home with you (as well as those who visit on occasion), and to enhance the value and resale potential of your home, there are many things that can be done — some by you if you feel up to it, or by others you can engage. The majority of these changes and treatments are going to universal design.

We'll start by looking at and discussing those features, concepts, treatments, and design elements that are relatively simple and inexpensive that often can be done without a building permit, inspection, or any demolition or construction. This means minimal dust and mess also.

If you are so inclined and feel comfortable in attempting the repairs yourself, you can do many of these, or have your children or a friend do them for you.

In fact, other than knowing that something has been added, moved, changed, or removed from what was there previously, no one will ever know any work was done. This is the great thing about universal design improvements — they just fit in.

The next day, your home will look like it has always been that way. Some items may be a little shinier or newer looking than the others, but that would likely be the only reason they would stand out.

So we'll start with those easy fixes that involve switches of various types and functions, drawer pulls, door knobs and locks, and lighting.

Then we'll move on from there to items that are going to require some construction (and possibly some demolition) and will be a little more disruptive or possibly create some minor inconvenience to you and the others in your home than the simple fixes — until they are completed.

Existing plumbing fixtures, major appliances, flooring, cabinetry, windows, wall mounted controls, electric outlets, towel bars, mirrors, and similar items will be addressed — along with things such as grab bars, other kitchen and bathroom features, auxiliary lighting, and items for the exterior of your home.

All of these are going to be from a universal design approach that creates comfort, safety, accessibility, ease of use, and convenience for everyone in your home regardless of their physical size or ability.

3

Easy Universal Design Solutions

What Makes Design Solutions Easy?

There are several changes that you can make in your current home to make it more comfortable, safe, convenient, or accessible that require nothing more than taking out what is there and replacing it with a more suitable product or item — or simply removing it and doing without it. Essentially anyone can do it.

As a homeowner or renter, you or someone in your family can do it. A neighbor or friend can do it. A handyman can do it. A remodeler, contractor, or builder can do it.

These changes make a big, noticeable improvement, but they require no building permit or inspection. A little care is required, but they are easy to accomplish — depending on who does them and the number of tasks.

These modifications cover aspects of electrical, plumbing, lighting, doors, and cabinets.

Some other changes that I will suggest as we go along will require some light construction and may mean a little dust, localized mess, and temporary disruption in a particular room or area of the home.

You just need to make sure that whoever does the work in your home — if it's not you or someone you know and trust very well — that it is a properly authorized and licensed activity for the person performing the work and that they have all of their insurance policies in force (general liability, worker's compensation, and builder's risk). Make them show you proof of insurance.

Lever Door Handles

When I think of universal design, lever door handles are one of the first items that comes to mind. This is true for any age, but I think seniors will get a great benefit from this feature.

These are the epitome of universal design. This concept provides safety, comfort, and convenience.

The use of the lever style door handle on any solid door that opens in or out — including storm doors, screen doors, entrance doors, patio doors, and interior doors, whether or not they have locks or dead bolts — allow the very young and the very old to use them successfully.

This includes young people who are so short as to be barely able reach the handles with outstretched fingers (such as your grandchildren or the children of your immediate neighbors) to those with weakened hand or arm strength or severe range-of-motion limitations who may have difficulty extending their hands or using their fingers to grasp things such as a traditional door knob.

What makes the lever handle such an ideal universal design element is the way it can be operated and the door released to open in several different ways.

It has a large tolerance for error and requires low physical effort to use.

Unlike a traditional door knob, this doesn't need to be grasped with the entire hand or turned with the hand. Therefore, it doesn't take any particular amount of strength to hold onto or turn it.

It can be used with the full hand to operate it (even with arthritis or a hand that has trouble making a fist because grasping and turning are not part of the way this handle is used), just a couple of fingers to push down on it, the side of the hand (open or in a fist) to push on it, the back of the hand or wrist to push down, the elbow or forearm to push down, the sides of both hands together to apply enough release pressure when your hands are messy or when you're holding something that you can't put down easily (or supporting yourself on a cane or walker), or even with a box or something else you might be holding to push down on the lever.

This obviously accommodates the full range of ages and many different types of physical abilities, but it has the added practical benefit of being able to be operated when your hands are full with something you really don't want to set down or can't put down easily — or when your hands might be messy or greasy and you'd rather not grasp the lever and then have to go back later and clean it. Your hands might also be supporting you on a cane or walker.

From a safety standpoint, the levers (unlike traditional rounded knobs) can be operated successfully while wearing a heavy glove or mitten or while using a towel to prevent transfer of whatever you might have on your hands.

From an aesthetic standpoint, the lever handles provide a nice sleek, clean, modern, contemporary look and are available in several styles, finishes, and colors — with and without locks.

For those that want an immediate solution without replacing every door knob in the home, the rounded knobs can be fitted with a device — also available in various colors and finishes — that adapts the knobs to look and function like a lever handle.

Conversely, a lockset and door handle that is the opposite of universal design and accessibility is the thumb-latch style entry lockset. You shouldn't have any of these in your home. While they may be attractive because they remind us of an earlier time, they aren't practical.

This type of lockset often requires tremendous dexterity and thumb pressure (or pressing down with the side of your hand to depress the latch) to hold it down long enough to disengage it from the striker plate and jamb.

This is often a two-handed operation — depressing the latch with one hand and holding it that way while grasping the handle and pulling or pushing the door open with the other — and presents challenges to many people in using it. There is not much tolerance for error in using this.

If you have such a lockset anywhere in your home, you'll want to replace it with the single lever handle — even if you personally can operate it right now. Think visitability and the abilities of others in your home.

With universal design, it no longer is a matter of some people having the strength, agility, coordination, or balance to operate something while someone else may struggle with it. It needs to be safe, comfortable, and easy for all to use it.

Rocker Light Switches

I also think of the rocker or "Decora" brand light switches when I think of universal design.

These and the lever style door handles top the list of universal design features for me. Literally, anyone who can reach or touch this style of light switch can use it.

Both the door handle and the light switch offer a component of safety, comfort, and convenience in being able to use them so flexibly.

Both require low physical effort and can accommodate a wide tolerance for error.

You can push on the light switch in the middle or on any other part of it. It will turn on or off, as needed without pushing it "exactly right."

You can use one finger, the tip of a finger, the flat of your hand, a fist, the side of your hand, the back of your hand, your wrist, your elbow, your shoulder, or even an object that you might be holding in your hand — basically anything that provides enough contact and pressure to move the switch into the on or off position.

Again, if you are holding something, holding onto something, steadying or balancing yourself (with a cane or walker, for instance), or your hands are dirty and you don't want to make a mark on the switch, switchplate, or wall, the rocker or Decora switch is great.

Contrast this with the tiny toggle-style switch that typically must be grasped or pushed with more physical effort and with greater accuracy that the rocker switches — there is no comparison.

In terms of aesthetics, the rocker or Decora switches provide a clean, modern, contemporary look, while the toggle switches look a little old-fashioned.

The rocker switches are a great universal design solution, but in many ways they are just the accepted style to use. They definitely fit in and are probably more noticeable today when they aren't used than when they are.

Illuminated Light Switches

A small but important modification for light switches (for the rocker or Decora style) is getting them with a small light in them that makes them easy to find in dim light, in darkened rooms, or at night.

They're great for your guests and visitors, too.

Simply take out the existing rocker switches and replace them with these or do this as you are replacing the old-style toggle switches.

This adds safety and convenience — plus the comfort of knowing that the light switch can be located.

Motion Sensor Light Switches

In swapping out light switches from toggle to rocker or Decora — or even if the rocker or Decora switches are already in place — a motion sensor (also called motion detector or movement sensor) light switch that mounts in the same space as the switch it is replacing can provide peace-of-mind and added safety as well as convenience in low traffic areas.

The switch turns on any light that is controlled by it — ceiling fixture or switched lamp (plugged into a wall outlet controlled by that switch) with incandescent, florescent, LED, or halogen bulbs — and stays on for either a fixed period of time or for a time that can be set to turn off the lights after the sensor detects no movement in the room.

When you enter a darkened room — such as a powder room or guest bedroom — with something in your hands to put away in that room (paper goods, towels, linens, or clean laundry) you can take care of your mission without being concerned about locating or using the light switch. This works great for visitors and guests also.

If you are using a cane, walker, or wheelchair — or this applies to someone else in your home, or possibly a guest or visiting relative — this saves moving to where the light switch is located and then actually using the light switch to illuminate the room.

This also provides a measure of security by having lights that come on as if someone in the home has turned them on — when someone or something not expected to be present is detected.

Even if you are home but are not in that part of your home, this is a tremendous safety and security feature for you because it will look from the outside like you responded to the noise.

For exterior lighting, fixtures are available that are solar powered so they literally can be placed anywhere — on the fascia, on a pole, on a fence, on a porch railing or post, on the garage — without needing electric wiring to run them. This adds to your security, safety, and peace-of-mind.

They turn on when the motion sensor is activated, and they are powered by solar energy. The solar collectors just need to be mounted where they get direct sunlight during the day to recharge.

Timer Light Switches

A similar idea for switching on and off lights at pre-determined times but with a little less flexibility than having a light come on when you enter a room and turn off when you leave is to use an electric timer that plugs into an electrical outlet.

These are inexpensive switches that can be used anywhere in your home where you want lights to come on regularly at the same time. They allow one or more lamps to plug into the timer and be turned on and off at fixed times that you determine and set.

You can change the activation times as daylight hours get longer or shorter, and there is an override switch when you want to turn the light on even when it is scheduled to be off. The timer works well for operating holiday, outdoor, or decorative lighting also.

Be aware that when the power goes off, the timer will be affected so check it periodically to make sure it reflects the correct time — also adjust it an hour forward or back for the semi-annual time change.

Photo Cell Light Switches

This is another alternative that you can use for exterior lighting and indoor lamps (for safety, security, comfort, and convenience) that only need to be on at night. Instead of relying on a manual switch or an electric timer, a photo cell can be used to turn the lights on when you need them at night.

It can be part of the light fixture or a separate sensor switch that is screwed into the light socket with the bulb then screwed into it.

The sensor will turn the lights on that it controls when the ambient lighting has dropped to a low enough level to require the lights to come on. It's a timer of sorts — one operated by daylight. They do wear out occasionally and need to be replaced, but they do not require any other maintenance.

The lights will stay on until sufficient daylight causes them to turn off. However, they sometimes will come on and remain on when the sky is very cloudy or during a heavy rain or snowfall.

The important thing to remember is to aim the photo cell sensors away from other lights that might interfere with their sensory ability.

Programmable/Preset Light Switches

This is another safety, convenience, and efficiency option available for you to include in your home. You can have your lights come on with a sensor or turn them on manually with the light switch, but a device that will fit into a standard switch box can be used to have lights come on and stay on for a preset fixed period of time (for instance 5 or 10 minutes).

It also can be programmed by you to stay on for a certain period of time before turning off the lights (say 20 or 30 minutes). These aren't affected by movement.

For any of these devices that I have discussed for controlling when the lights come on or turn off, there are several manufacturers, models, styles, sources, and price points available — as well as places where you can find them.

Digital Thermostats

This solution is similar to the light switch improvements for additional convenience and comfort, and it allows anyone in the home to access and use the device. That's what makes it universal.

It's just a matter of taking out a manual, dial-type or slide-switch style mercury thermostat and replacing it with one that has a digital display — programmable or not.

Some digital thermostats have the ability to be set and to control temperatures for various times of the day or for multiple days. Some just maintain the temperature as it is set — for heating or cooling — until changed.

Either way, they can be read from a few feet away and don't rely on grasping a dial or switch and trying to move it a small amount.

Some can even be controlled remotely from smartphones and tablets.

Obviously, this is good for all ages and even people with some vision or coordination difficulties.

It is certainly much easier to read the display with a specific temperature number than trying to determine the settings and temperature on a non-digital one since the numbers are larger and are usually lit on the digital type — it's also easier to set the precise desired temperature and save money in the process.

The thermostat is easily changed out by you as the homeowner or renter (or a friend, neighbor, or relative), but it also can be done by a handyman or remodeler as part of a larger project.

It can be replaced exactly where is has been, but an even better strategy is to move it to a lower position so it is more accessible and visible to everyone.

This will require a little more work to move the wiring so the first step would be just to replace the old thermostat with a digital one. Then it can be lowered later to a more accessible position.

This way it is comfortable for you to use and access — even while using a walker or wheelchair — or for your visiting grandchildren to access and use when you request their help.

Door/Drawer Pulls

Opening doors and drawers throughout the home in kitchens, bathrooms, laundry rooms, and elsewhere may be an issue for people with small hands, weak hand or arm strength, or arthritis in their hands or fingers. They may have trouble grasping and using the door and drawer pulls or handles.

It's not just on cabinet doors and drawers but on dressers, night stands, end tables, armoires, and other furniture as well.

In order to make it easier for everyone to use them, this one universal design change can make a huge difference.

In addition to making it easier, more comfortable, more accessible, and safer for everyone to use, replacing the door and drawer knobs and pulls can really dress up the appearance of a kitchen or bath (or furniture) and give it a modern look.

Depending on which hardware is selected and the number of cabinet drawers and doors in the kitchen, bathrooms, laundry room, garage, basement, and elsewhere in the home, it may not be an inexpensive change but one that is easily done. It can even be done a little at a time if this is something you are going to be doing yourself.

This certainly can be done by homeowners and renters.

It also can be done by a handyman or during a kitchen or bath makeover.

What you want to achieve are door and drawer handles and pulls that require little-to-no gripping strength to operate — unlike that needed for using small knobs that have to be grasped before they can be leveraged to open the door or drawer.

Also, you want plenty of room to insert your fingers into the pull rather than just your fingertips so you reduce the risk of your hand slipping off and assuring that you actually can open the door or drawer.

Some people even like the idea of using a folded leather strap attached to the door as a pull on a pantry or other large door that can be grabbed or used by inserting your hand into it.

Whatever approach you decide to take, your existing door and drawer pulls can easily be switched out by removing them and attaching the new ones with the same mounting holes — as long as you select new ones that have the two mounting posts 3" apart like the ones you are replacing.

Pulls that require wider mounting holes than 3" will require drilling new holes and possibly patching and touching up the existing ones.

For the knobs that have just a single mounting bolt, a second hole (or sometimes two holes to achieve a center alignment) will need to be drilled.

This is easily done by creating a template out of paper, cardboard, or thin wood to get all of the holes in the same place on the various doors and drawer fronts. Just align it in the same place on every door or drawer.

Again, some patching and touchup might be required for the unused former holes.

The major safety concern for existing and new pulls is that any material on the pull surface that sticks out past the main part of the pull can catch clothing or skin when someone walks by too closely or comes in contact with it.

An alternate to using door pulls is to use magnetic latches that hold a door closed and then release it by depressing the lock slightly with the door front to release the lock and allow it to "pop" open.

This eliminates any issues that someone might have with hand or arm strength or range-of-motion in pulling open a cabinet door.

Just a pushing motion on the door will release the latch and allow the door to open.

Additionally, some doors also will remain closed with tension or spring assisted hinges or just the weight of the door without using a catch to secure it — and open by grasping a corner or edge of the door and gently pulling on it.

Such doors typically do not have a door pull and provide a cleaner, more uniform look that way.

The issue with doors that have no pulls on them — or don't use pulls to release the latch and open the doors — is that they aren't as intuitive to use and may be confusing for guests or visitors.

Still, they are common enough in usage that someone likely has seen them elsewhere and generally can figure out how to use them.

Single-Lever Faucets

When I think of universal design, another one of the first items that comes to mind is the single-lever faucet — for safety, comfort, accessibility, and convenience.

This is a classic example of universal design and one that is extremely functional as well as modern looking and visually appealing.

While it truly works for all ages and abilities, this is an excellent feature for seniors who might have issues with hand or arm strength, stamina, dexterity, coordination, balance, reach, range-of-motion, or insensitivity to feeling heat in their hands.

Because it is such a serviceable and attractive feature, it's already included in many homes just because of its appearance.

As a homeowner or renter, if you don't have the single-lever faucet already, you can easily swap out any existing dual-style or two-handle faucet set with the single-lever model if you have the tools and experience to do light plumbing work. If not, it's an easy project for a friend or relative to tackle.

The important thing to remember is removing all the residue and gaskets or putty from the existing installation and putting the new one in place on a clean, dry surface — using the new gaskets and putty as recommended in the instructions that come with the new faucet.

Of course, handymen, remodelers, or plumbers can do this as part of a larger project.

Just make sure the replacement faucet uses the same holes that are already present in the sink or countertop or that it completely covers and seals any of the unused ones. Don't leave any holes exposed.

The single-lever faucet is more stylish and contemporary than two-handle faucets, although fancy and rather expensive two-handle faucet sets are available.

That really isn't the point — how fancy or expensive they are. Aside from offering a sleek, modern look, the single-lever faucet offers significant safety benefits over the two-handle style.

The single-lever faucet can be operated by anyone who can reach it — without being overly concerned about someone accidently burning or hurting themselves by getting hot water unexpectedly.

The faucet handle and mixer would have to be positioned all the way to the far left and have the hot water come on rather instantly for this to be a concern.

Contrast that with someone using a sink with two faucet handles and not paying attention, realizing, or understanding that the left side is the hot water control and being indifferent to the water temperature as long as they were able to have water coming out — until it may be too late to avoid discomfort or a mild burn.

A safety benefit that the single-lever faucet affords that likely everyone can appreciate and relate to is being able to use it while you are preparing food.

After handling raw meat or fish or having sauces or something sticky or messy on your hands, you can turn on the faucet and have the water come on without touching the handle directly with your affected hands (and transferring whatever is on your hands to the faucet handle). In fact, there are several ways of activating the lever without actually grabbing or holding it.

The same is true when your hands are dirty, oily, muddy, or greasy from doing other work around the house or yard — or if your hands are holding onto a cane or walker for balance or support as you are trying to turn on the water.

Depending on the type and size of the lever, you can turn on the faucet with your forearm, fist, wrist, back of your hands, elbows, your hands while wearing kitchen gloves or using a towel you are holding to avoid direct contact, a wooden spoon or other kitchen utensil, or even a bowl or pot you might be holding.

This flexibility in use and low physical effort are hallmarks of universal design.

There also are faucets available now that just require some type of light contact along the spout to activate the water flow (and turn it off again) — less intuitive for a guest of visitor but very convenient for those accustomed to using it. However the valve does need to remain on and the temperature setting pre-selected for this to work.

Generally, the water temperature is more consistent with a single-lever faucet than the two-handle system when the water is turned off and then back on again because the temperature mixing does not have to be redone.

Although the water is subject to cooling off — depending on the length of time that has passed since the single-lever faucet was last used (and the distance from the hot water heater) — the water is relatively the same temperature as it was when it was turned off (or it soon will be as soon as the hot water flows back to it).

With a two-handle faucet system, the water has to be remixed by turning on each handle and then testing the water temperature until it feels about the way it was previously — unless it had been turned on with only cold or only hot water.

Someone with balance, coordination, range-of-motion, and other limitations, will likely find using two-faucets to be more difficult — aside from the safety and convenience benefit of using the single-lever faucet.

To make sure that you or someone else in your home doesn't accidentally turn on the hot water when you or they didn't intend to or expect it, a universal design gadget that you may want to get or request — for those spouts that will accept them — is a screw-on adapter in the place of a typical aerator that provides a blue light (for cold water) or red light (for hot water) to the water stream to indicate its relative temperature.

This non-electric light doesn't present any type of shock concern (it is battery operated and is reflected into the water stream to create the illusion of colored water), and it is an immediate visual clue for the general water temperature as well as great fun for the grandkids and a conversation starter when guests are present.

Another option is selecting a faucet that already has a built-in light to indicate the relative temperature. There are several that do this.

Single-lever faucets should be used throughout the home — kitchens (including islands), baths (including powder rooms), laundry rooms, mud rooms, garages, summer kitchens, wet bars, patios, and basements.

One additional safety, comfort, and convenience issue to remember involves the choice of the faucet spout to provide enough room to get your hands under the flowing water and also to reduce splashing and spray.

Some faucets are very compact and have very short spouts. It is hard to get your hands or a dish, plate, glass, or pot totally under the water stream without contacting the back of the sink.

Make sure the spout is long enough to deliver the water stream a comfortable distance away from the back of the sink, or you won't be able to use it effectively.

Another consideration with the faucet spout is excess spray or splash from a spout that is designed too tall or high (resulting in a lot of splash or water bounce off the bottom of the sink to the surrounding countertop, floor, or whoever is using the sink). Also, some faucets are angled or contoured to the point that water tends to hit the bottom of the sink and refract directly out onto the person using it.

Both cases present safety, comfort, and convenience issues.

Shallow bowls and vessel sinks (because of their shape) tend to create more splash issues than others.

Instant Hot/Drinking Water Faucets

There are two other types of faucets that often are found at the sink that can present safety issues. In general, they are installed for comfort and convenience, but this can backfire without exercising due caution.

The first is found in the kitchen at the main sink although it could be found at a kitchen island sink, wet bar sink, or outdoor kitchen sink. This is an instant hot water dispenser used for making hot tea, instant coffee, hot chocolate, or an instant cup of soup. It can be used for dissolving gelatin or for cooking when very hot water is needed.

It is activated by a single lever (turned, lifted. or depressed by pushing down on it), but there is no temperature adjustment at the point of delivery. This needs to be adjusted under the sink. As such, the water is delivered — steaming hot — when the faucet is opened.

By design, it is universal in that everyone who is tall enough to reach it and access it can turn it on and use it.

The issue is one of safety. While it provides a measure of convenience (instead of waiting while water heats on the cooktop or stove, or in the microwave), if the water is hot enough to do what it is intended to do (up to 200 degrees), it can mildly injure someone who accidentally places their hand under the stream, has the very hot water splash on their skin, or is taken off-guard when the heat transfer through the cup or vessel is more than expected.

The safety concerns may not outweigh the convenience benefits, but extreme care needs to be exercised in installing and using this feature.

For seniors with cognitive issues or younger grandchildren who may not appreciate the heat produced and thus not handle the liquid safely, or for those with balance, hand strength, or coordination issues that might tend to spill the very hot liquid, this fixture should not be installed or allowed to remain without the proper amount of caution.

Setting the temperature on the unit lower might help reduce the burning risk, but it might have to be too low for the hot water to be useful.

The second type of convenience faucet is a spout or spigot at the sink just for filling a drinking glass or drinking from directly.

This is universal in design and application as long as everyone in your home can activate the faucet lever.

The only concern is water that might splash from the sink onto the person using the water tap — or onto the countertop or floor. This could create a minor inconvenience and possibly a slipping hazard until the errant water was cleaned up.

Pot-Fillers

Another type of single lever faucet that is often used in the kitchen is the pot filler. This is found in new construction and in recently remodeled homes.

If your home does not have one, it probably doesn't need to have one installed. The safety concerns outweigh the convenience issues for this one.

I caution against using pot fillers — not so much because of what they are but how they are used. It is not a universal design strategy and can create unforeseen and unpleasant issues for the homeowner.

It typically is located in the backsplash above the stove or cooktop — although I have seen them on an island, at an auxiliary sink, or at the main sink.

Again, the issue is one of safety.

A pot filler certainly supplies convenience — being able to fill a stockpot, double boiler, saucepan, or any other cooking vessel right from the cooking surface without having to carry it to the stove or cooktop from the sink.

Just take an empty pot to the stove or cooktop, add water from the pot filler, and turner on the burner.

What happens that makes it unsafe and keeps it from being a universal design strategy is that it gives people a false sense of well-being.

They are struck by the convenience of filling their cooking vessel right at the stove or cooktop and don't relate the weight of the water to what they are doing.

Since they are not filling the pot or pan at the sink and then walking with it over to the stove or cooktop (whatever the distance is), they are disconnected from the process and have no idea how much it might weigh or if they can pick it up or move it again after they are done using it — even if only some of the liquid remains.

After the cooking is complete, they may find that they cannot lift the pot from a waist-high or higher level on the stove or cooktop — because of their short height, hand or arm strength, reach, shoulder or elbow joint issues, range-of-motion limitations, the volume and weight of the liquid (water weighs 8 pounds per gallon before anything is added to the pot or pan), the height of the cooking surface, or a combination of several of these.

They risk spilling or splashing it on themselves or the floor, knocking over or dropping the pot, or hurting themselves as they strain to lift something relatively heavy at an awkward height.

They may find that they will need to bail the liquid into smaller containers before being able to lift the pot.

There are the additional safety issues of needing to reach (possibly over a hot or warm burner that may be in use) to access the pot filler, and having a water source over the stove that could drip if not shut off properly or splash if turned on too much while filling.

When grandchildren want to help out in the kitchen, they are not going to be able to access the pot filler or move the heavy pot unless they are tall teen-agers.

This fixture is modern and attractive, but because of the safety and accessibility issues concerned with using it, you should skip this. If you already have one, leave it unless you are doing a major kitchen remodel. You just won't find yourself using it much.

Pipe Wrapping

One more issue concerning the plumbing in your home that you can handle easily — or have it done easily — is wrapping the water pipes and the traps under the sinks.

This is a safety concern for members of your household and for guests.

It's not so much that people can injure or burn themselves from direct contact with the hot water pipes in your home. They can, but the hot water is not present in the pipes at temperature except when the faucet is open and hot water is being delivered at a particular fixture.

Hot water is not present in the waste traps under the sinks for very long because most of it flows out, and the little of it that remains in the pipes cools quickly.

The real concern is that you or someone else might bang into the pipes with an arm or leg and suffer a bruise or cut. This is a particular concern for those with reduced feeling in their legs, ankles, and feet.

That's why the water pipes and the traps under the sinks should be wrapped — to cushion and soften any contact that someone might have with them.

This would be especially true for someone in a wheelchair using a sink that was accessible to them.

Interior Painting

In most cases, painting walls, trim, and ceilings is something that you as the homeowner or renter can accomplish — depending on how big the job is, how high the ceilings are, and your balance, coordination, stamina, and ability to use your arms and legs to reach or climb ladders.

Hiring a professional painter, handyman, decorator, or remodeler is certainly a way to go for people who don't feel up to tackling the task themselves or want it done quickly with no mess or cleanup to worry about.

There are three issues to consider about painting.

First, if you are concerned about indoor air quality or that characteristic paint smell that goes along with such a project, look for and select low- or no-VOC paint (volatile organic compounds). They are more money than paint that contains higher amounts of VOC, but it will eliminate the strong vapors that often go along with painting. Finding low-VOC paint is not difficult.

Second, if you have a popcorn ceiling as a surface finish anywhere in your home, it may have asbestos in it. As long as you don't disturb it, you are fine. As you go to paint it, you could loosen some of it. Have your ceiling checked before beginning if you are unsure as to whether it contains asbestos and if it might be an air quality issue for you.

Third, if your home was built in 1977 or earlier, it falls under the Lead Paint Rule of the EPA. You should engage a professional to test your air quality for lead particles before painting or remodeling just to be safe.

You may have lead paint present, or you may not. The air quality test will tell if there is lead residue in your home.

You may need to rely on a professional remodeling or painting service for this work in your home.

Push Button/Keypad Entry Door Locks

Here is a practical solution that affords additional safety, security, convenience, and peace-of-mind.

Replace existing entry door locksets with a push button or keypad lock system.

Make sure to get a lockset with a lever handle.

Simply take the lockset out that is there and replace it with the keypad lockset. There are different colors and finishes available.

This design works for all ages, but get a keypad with the largest numbers possible to make it easier to read and to be able to touch the keys without difficulty.

If you have young grandchildren who can be trusted with the combination, they can unlock the door by pressing the correct numbers or letters. There is no worry of them losing a key or for you trying to keep track of how many people have been issued keys.

Everyone in the household (or those to whom you grant access) can unlock the door by just punching in the correct combination of letters, numbers, or pattern, and the lock can be reprogrammed as often as desired for additional security.

This is great for your extended family (or trusted neighbors) that may visit regularly but not live at your address. It also allows someone to enter your home to check on you when you may have fallen or otherwise aren't answering your door or phone.

Remembering a combination could be an issue with people who have short-term memory loss, but then using a key to unlock the door is likely an issue as well.

An additional safety and security benefit of the keypad lock is that it can be programmed with a separate combination for temporary access each time repair and service technicians or personnel need to enter your home — so that the actual combination is not handed out or revealed and there is no need to have a key given to them or hidden outside for them.

Of course, you can reprogram the lock as often as you feel comfortable in doing so. Just make sure to let everyone who needs access to your home what the new combination is (and be sure to write it down where you can find it again later).

4

More Extensive And Intensive Universal Design Solutions

Going To The Next Level

In addition to the several changes we just looked at that require hardly any work in your home other than swapping out less efficient or effective light switches, door handles, cabinet and drawer handles and pulls, and faucets, there are several other changes that you should consider to make your home more comfortable, safe, convenient, or accessible that require some advance planning and some professional help.

Unless you are very skilled in doing some of this work yourself as a homeowner, you are going to require the help of contractors to help you accomplish the design strategies and solutions that I discuss in this chapter.

Some construction and demolition (and dust) will likely be required to complete these changes. That's why it may take the work of professionals to accomplish it.

Nevertheless, these are the types of solutions and changes that you should consider as part of a comprehensive, sensible universal design approach to creating a safe, comfortable, and accessible home.

Depending on the complexity of the changes and the extent of them, they might be able to be accomplished without a building permit or inspection.

These changes will make a big, noticeable impact on the general safety and comfort of your living space.

However, in keeping with the objective of universal design about having the changes as invisible as possible, they won't necessarily be obvious to those not familiar with the way your home looked before the changes were made.

Open Doorways

A great universal design solution that is aesthetic, sustainable, and practical is creating the illusion of a doorway for dividing space or separating rooms.

This design technique, that doesn't actually include an operating door, is used frequently as an architectural element, and you can use it as part of your overall universal design strategy for both style and function.

These open doorways can be nearly as wide as the hallway or space they are framing.

On long entry halls that take people from the front of your home to the back, such a feature (sometime with a glass or decorative transom over it) can be used to define the separation of the front of the house from the back, but no door needs to be mounted because there is no need to close off the space.

Archway passages as entrances to a master suite vestibule or a secondary bedroom wing function the same way. They act as a doorway but remain open at all times because there is no door attached to them. The doorway is implied rather than actually created.

In the same way, they can also be used as entrances for dining rooms or family rooms or other areas in your home to indicate where the spaces begin but are totally open and accessible.

These open passageways allow wide, unrestricted access and passage by anyone in your home and facilitate movement of furniture as well because there is a doorway but no door. Thus, they can be wide.

In terms of accessibility and visitability, these create the illusion of a doorway but do not restrict passage.

36" Doorways

This is another one of the items that tops my list of features when I think of universal design.

It is such an intuitive solution, but it has yet to be embraced by the majority of the nation's homebuilders. Therefore, most homes do not have them.

If more homes came with 36" doorways (the size of the actual door itself rather than the finished opening which generally is somewhat smaller) already included, homeowners would not have to incur the time, expense, and inconvenience (regardless of who does the work) of replacing the existing doors with larger ones.

Unless 36" interior doorways (or "3-0" as they are called in construction for a 3'-0" doorway) are specifically requested by new home purchasers in semi-custom or custom homes, most of the new homes being built are designed with 32" or smaller doorways (called "2-8" in construction terminology for 2'-8" or 32").

The difference in wall and floor space between a 32" and 36" doorway is 4", but that is a very important 4" for universal design and accessibility.

The practical reason for all interior doorways being 36" wide — many exterior doorways already are 36" (or larger when double doors are used) — is for ease of moving furniture about in the home.

Anyone who has ever moved a mattress or bed frame into a bedroom — or other furniture from room-to-room in a home or apartment — knows how challenging it can be dealing with a 32" or smaller doorway compared to one that is 36".

Skinned knuckles, bruised shins, and dinged furniture — or even getting furniture stuck or wedged into the doorway opening — have resulted from narrow doorways.

It's sometimes hard enough to deal with a 36" or 3-feet doorway, but that is so much better than smaller ones. Anything larger than 36" such as 40" (while being helpful) would be noticeable and contrary to our universal design objective of creating invisible and unobtrusive solutions, treatments, and improvements.

However, just giving everyone an easier time of moving furniture or other items about between rooms in the home or apartment is reason enough for having the wider 36" doorways.

The visitability factor comes into play when we note that a wheelchair may need 29" or more of clearance —

with a 32" width being the published design guideline —
just to negotiate safely through a doorway.

While a 32" doorway is wide enough in theory to
accommodate wheelchair access for someone living in
your home (or an occasional visitor), it doesn't measure
up. Taking into account a door thickness of 1⅜" or
more (1¾" for a solid core door), a hinge of another ¾"
or so, and the stop (nearly another ⅜"), the effective
clearance in a 32" doorway has been reduced by some
2½" or more.

In order to achieve a true 32" or larger effective
passageway for easy wheelchair access in a home, 36"
doors are the minimum size that should be used. A few
inches wider would be even better, but 36" doorways
are currently the widest size commonly available.

In some cases, pocket doors — mounted inside the walls
— or sliding doors (also called "barn doors") — hung
along the inside or outside walls of the doorway — may
provide a wider effective opening as well.

Mounting pocket doors inside the walls will require
some demolition and construction — and possibly
moving some electric wiring and light switches.

Surface mounted doors do not require any major
construction as long as they don't cover a light switch or
wall outlet — just installing the track and hanging the

door along with removing the stop, striker plate, hinges, and casing from the door jamb and then patching as required to leave a smooth opening.

This may be a larger job than you are willing to tackle on your own, and a handyman or remodeler can be used.

To swap out the 32" or smaller door with the 36" door, it's often just a matter of removing the 32" ("2-8") or smaller doorway (door, jamb, and molding), enlarging the opening, and then replacing it with a larger one — making sure it is plumb and square so it opens freely.

The drywall needs to be trimmed — or cutout and then replaced, patched, and painted to allow for a wider opening — and the doorway needs to be reframed to make this happen. Wiring and light switches may have to be moved as well.

This can be a do-it-yourself project but is more easily accomplished by a handyman, carpenter, or remodeling contractor.

For doorways at the end of hallways that cannot be enlarged without first making the hallways wider, this should be done by a remodeler when undertaking a more comprehensive project.

To widen the hallways, the space will need to be taken from the rooms bordering the hallway.

Wider Hallways

This idea goes along with 36" doorways but takes a lot more planning and work to accomplish.

This is not a matter of just removing a door and making the opening larger. This requires moving walls on either side of the hallway — at least one and likely two or more — depending on how it's configured.

A typical interior hallway in a home is 36" or less, and that obviously can't accommodate a 36" doorway at the end of the hallway or comfortable passage along the hallway by anyone in a wheelchair or walker.

To make hallways wider, the rooms with a common wall with the hallway will necessarily be affected as space for the wider hallway will be taken from them.

Widening hallways requires tearing out existing walls and reconstructing them a few inches away from where they were and toward the adjacent space. Some wiring and possibly air conditioning or heating ductwork will have to be relocated also.

The ceiling and flooring in the hallway will need to be redone or repaired as the space is widened into the original wall area where no ceiling or floor treatment existed (the walls were there and the surfaces will be in their untreated, original state).

Hallways that are 42-45" in width seem to be field-tested and reasonable. Adding wall blocking (adaptable design discussed on page 178) inside the hallway walls as they are rebuilt will facilitate installation of grab bars or other devices and fixtures at a later date as a needs-specific solution.

This project will likely require the services of a handyman, remodeler, HVAC contractor, electrician, painter, flooring contractor, and air quality inspector — and a dumpster or some other way of removing the construction debris.

Door Swing

Occasionally, existing interior or exterior doors are mounted so that they open from the wrong side of the doorway opening or in the wrong direction (the way they swing open from their closed position) for the convenience, safety, and accessibility of those in the household.

This means that the hinges need to be switched left-for-right or right-for-left to allow the door to open more desirably and conveniently for you.

The amount of room near the latch or door handle side of the door and the room to approach it (whatever is comfortable for you and anyone else in your home but generally up to 24" of clear space to allow someone in a walker or wheelchair to be able to access the door handle) and open it easily also factor into deciding whether the door swing should be adjusted.

It could also be a matter of what the door opens into or onto in terms of floor area near the door, an adjacent wall, cabinets, fixtures, or furniture. Again, work to keep the approach zone by the door clear.

Reversing the swing from side to side, so that it opens opposite of where it is now but still in or out the same, requires a little work in terms of reversing the position of the hinges and striker plate and recess — plus patching, sanding, and painting where the hardware was before being moved.

Reversing whether the door opens in or out (except where local building codes require certain doors to open a particular way) requires a little more work. The stop and lockset have to be reversed also.

Unless you are particularly handy with woodworking, this is likely a job for professionals such as a handyman, carpenter, or a remodeling contractor.

Closet Doors

There are many different styles of closet doors, depending on what room the closet is located in and what the purpose of the closet is.

There are bedroom closets — both wall closets with bypass, hinged, or bi-fold doors (or maybe even an old-style accordion door with pleats in it that slides along a track) as well as walk-in closets with pocket, bi-fold, or hinged doors.

There are linen, coat, and utility closets in the hallway or foyer. There are linen closets in the bath. There is the pantry and possibly laundry closet space in the kitchen (sometimes the hallway).

The same comments about door swing apply to closets in terms of accessibility and ease of use. Make sure there is a clear approach zone by the side or sides of the closet where the door handle is located.

If there is a hinged door, it might open into the closet, or it could open out into the hallway or into the room in which it is located. Bi-fold doors will stack to the side of the opening and protrude into the room — narrowing the walking space around them.

Bi-fold doors can severely restrict the passageway around them when they are located in a hallway, so the hallway needs to be wide enough to accommodate an opened bi-fold door and still allow someone to walk past it in the remaining space behind it.

The same issue is present with a solid hinged door that opens out into the hallway.

Also, louvered bi-fold doors (the ones with slats in one or both halves of the door for ventilation and air flow) tend to attract dust and may present an indoor air quality or allergen issue for people susceptible to dust.

Because the closet door (hinged or bi-fold) must remain open while the closet is in use rather than just being opened to pass through it, or kept closed for privacy like many other doors in the home, take a hard look at how each door is used before deciding if they need to be changed or allowed to remain.

Evaluate the approach space to make sure that it is safe and adequate. Look at the way the door is opened and the impact it has on adjacent space or furniture while it remains in the open position.

See if there are any potential obstructions preventing the door from opening fully or allowing others in your home to walk past it while it is open, and assess how easy it is to open and close the door to gain access to the closet.

For in-line pantry, supply, broom, linen closets and other such tall vertical compartments that are part of the cabinetry, dividing the space into smaller sections with smaller doors is better so that the doors aren't so heavy. This way, just one area of the closet or pantry can be accessed as needed rather than opening and handling a large door to open the entire space.

If you still have any of the accordion-style vinyl or fabric doors that slide along a track and collapse to one side as they are opened, you will want to replace them with a bi-fold, bypass, or sliding door.

The accordion doors tend to bind in the track as they are being opened or closed, and it often requires two hands to operate them effectively.

Anyone in a wheelchair or using a walker or cane would find these doors difficult to use.

Bypass doors can be used when space is a concern and opening a door into a space may not be desirable. The concerns with bypass doors are that they restrict or limit access to just half of the closet at a time and they have a track on the floor in which the doors travel that could cause someone to catch their foot, walker, or wheelchair on it.

Again, if you are particularly handy with woodworking some of this can be accomplished by the homeowner, but this is likely a job for professionals such as a handyman, kitchen and bath designer, or a remodeling contractor.

Trench/Forward/Linear Drains

In a traditional bathtub — with or without a fixed shower head installation or a handheld shower that is used in addition to or in place of the shower head — the drain is located forward.

It is at the end of the tub — typically under the fill spout and the faucet handles or mixer and at the end opposite of where someone typically steps into the tub.

However, in a stall shower — either manufactured or constructed on site — the drain in the shower pan is located in or near the middle.

The floor of the shower is formed into an inverse pyramid with the drain at the center. Even when the floor of the shower is formed without using a manufactured pan, it is still constructed with the same design and shape.

I think the drain on a standard bathtub is in the correct spot for beneficial safety and comfort reasons and that most dedicated showers have it in the wrong place.

First, the function of a shower is to get clean by washing away dirt with soap and water. Do you really want to stand in used soapy water while it drains — sometimes quite slowly and hindered because you are standing on the drain?

Your feet and ankles never get totally clean until you move away from the drain — at the risk of slipping because you are walking in soapy water — and rinse them again after most of the water completely drains. Depending on how well and quickly the drain works, there can be a small pool of water around the drain.

Second, there is an uneven footing situation because of the way the floor slopes and pitches to the drain — from four different planes. This can be a slipping and balance issue.

Many times, you will actually be standing right on the drain which is not particularly comfortable and it can hinder the function of the drain.

For anyone using a transfer bench or shower chair, it is very hard to position it easily and keep it in one place.

Third, you often have to move about to try to get away from the water that is pooling at the drain, and this can result in slippery footing and potentially a dangerous fall.

Finally, if you want to stand on something such as a shower mat, a teak platform, or nonslip treads, these do not conform well to the inverse pyramid design and must be adapted to use them somewhat effectively and keep them from covering or blocking the drain.

The solution to this safety and comfort issue is to move the drain from the middle of the shower and put it back in the front like it is in the standard tub.

For homes built on a crawl space or basement, moving the drain a couple of feet is not a huge issue but will likely take professionals to do it.

A slab foundation takes more work and more expense to break up part of the concrete and move the drain (drains for multiple shower locations), but is worth it for the safety and comfort achieved. Of course the flooring will need to be repaired or replaced.

The drain is the main issue. The faucet, mixer, and shower head may be fine where they are.

To allow water to drain faster and provide a sleeker look to the shower, a trench or linear drain is recommended. The plumbing below the drain remains the same with just the way the water is collected on the surface changing.

There are even surface drains that look much like the flush deco-drains used on pool decks that come in a variety of finishes, colors, styles, and patterns.

Be sure to choose a design that will provide safe footing and not allow your foot or shower shoes to catch in any part of them.

The trench or linear drain that is located at the end of the shower ("forward"), with a flat shower floor gently pitched toward the drain, offers efficient draining and greater footing stability. Also, it accommodates the use of chairs, folding seats, or transfer benches in the shower. It also allows you to wear shower shoes if you like and to apply nonslip floor treatments easily.

Additionally, if someone else needs to be in the shower with you or someone else in your household to offer assistance, it is easier for them to stand and move about on a flat service and one without the water pooling in the center.

It will take a little demolition and the work of a cement mason, a tile setter, a plumber, a handyman, kitchen and bath designer, or a remodeler to accomplish this drain makeover unless you are very skilled and confident in tackling a job such as this.

Your overnight guests and the next owners of your home will thank you, too.

Zero-Step/No-Threshold/Barrier-Free Showers

When there is just a shower present in a bathroom with no bathtub, changing out the lip, threshold, transition, or step-up at the shower entrance to allow level access between the bathroom floor and the shower floor eliminates possible slipping or range-of-motion, balance, and coordination issues as someone steps from one surface to another — entering or leaving the shower — and allows free access to the shower by anyone.

It may look a little different than traditional showers that have a lip, step up, or raised shower pan, but this "zero-step" shower entrance is becoming more popular and eliminates many of the safety and access concerns normally present.

As you look around at other homes or hotels, you will see showers that have a step up of several inches from the bathroom floor into the shower (not as much as a bathtub but a sizeable step just the same). Then the reverse of this is true when exiting the shower — there can be a significant step down to the floor.

Actually the step down presents a safety concern because your foot likely is wet from the shower (even if you have mostly dried yourself in the shower) and you are placing it on a potentially slippery tile surface. A bath mat can still slip as you step on it.

This project can be done at the same time as the floor drain relocation and shower floor modification. It will take a little demolition and the work of a cement mason, a tile setter, a plumber, a handyman, or a remodeler to accomplish unless you are very skilled at tackling a job such as this in your own home.

Shower Glass Enclosures/Shower Doors

To keep as much water inside the tub or shower as possible while taking a shower or using the handheld shower, some people install shower doors or other glass panels. The glass is generally tempered (which crumbles into tiny pieces when it is shattered), and sometimes plexiglas is used instead of glass (which can be just as jagged and sharp as glass when it is broken).

Generally, a single hinged door is used for a walk-in or stall shower, and a two- or three-panel bypass set of doors is used for a tub.

The sliding bypass tub doors are mounted in a track that covers the bath opening, and they slide inside and along a top and bottom track to keep water from splashing outside the tub or shower and onto the bathroom floor.

The lower track is held in place with adhesive caulk and the weight of the two or three doors on top of it. The side tracks are fastened to the walls or sides of the bath/shower area with screws or wall fasteners. The top track simply rests in place atop the two sides and has the weight of the doors (rolling along a track inside it) keeping it in place.

Just adding the extra height and width of the lower track is enough to create a potential tripping hazard or entrance barrier for those people with balance or coordination issues, those with relatively short legs, and those with range-of-motion issues in the hips, ankles, or knees.

One-piece shower doors for stall showers typically open out into the room and generally have magnetic or ball closures that open rather easily and allow most anyone to use them.

However, they can easily release and pop open when fallen against or used for support during a slip — increasing the likelihood of a more serious fall and injury.

If they have a locking mechanism strong enough to prevent opening with incidental or light contact, they can create a safety hazard of a different nature and not be suitable for use by those not strong enough to operate the door.

They also can impact the area of approach and clearance around the shower as sufficient space needs to be allowed for people to open the door freely — and for the doors left or moved into in the open position not to obstruct access to anything else in the bathroom.

Regular cleaning and maintenance of the glass or plexiglas panels to keep soap scum and mildew from forming or building up on the surface is important from a cleanliness and appearance standpoint. However, it can also be a safety issue in the shower space.

When the bypass doors — and even the clear glass panels that are often used as walls or dividers along with shower doors to define the wet space and prevent water from getting into the rest of the room when the shower is used — have soap or other build-up on their surfaces, they can become slippery.

Then, when the slippery surfaces are touched or leaned against (especially when they are wet or you are wet) — from incidental contact to being used to try to keep from falling after a slip or loss of balance — they will hasten rather than hinder a more serious fall.

Depending on how they are installed and the type of glass or plexiglas used, the panels may not be able to support someone's weight or withstand a fall into it in a panic situation such as loss of balance, a slip, or fall.

If these glass panels were to break, flex, or dislodge from their mounts or supports, a more serious accident than just a fall could result. Even a serious cut could happen.

Additionally, the glass doors and glass panels can reflect and refract light in a way that creates glare and affects orientation, depth perception, or the ability to tell where objects are located.

Glare can obscure some objects (potentially causing injury by walking into something that isn't clearly visible), and it can cause some surfaces to appear wet even when they aren't. Glare is a real safety concern.

Many of the shower door or shower area panels also have towel bars attached to them or bolted onto or through holes drilled in them, which — in a panic situation — are used as grab bars and may break, pull loose, or cause the doors or panels to come out of their tracks or otherwise fail to offer the support required.

In general, there are so many reasons of a safety, convenience, comfort, and accessibility nature for not using glass or plexiglas around a shower or bath area and not that many good ones that support their use.

Why use a product that is known to cause injury — directly when a cut results from broken glass or indirectly if a fall results from failure of the panels or towel bars to support someone — when you aren't wearing clothing that would at least offer minimal protection?

It will take a little demolition and the work of a handyman, kitchen and bath designer, or a remodeler to accomplish removing the glass doors and panels unless you are a very skilled homeowner in tackling a job such as this. They should not be part of your bathroom remodeling. Wet rooms and other strategies are much safer.

Removing the glass panels or doors will be awkward, and they may be heavy. They could have sharp edges. Also, they will need to be disposed of in some way.

Wet Room/Shower Room

If you have a relatively small bathroom, or you are working with redesigning one, creating a zero-step shower entrance presents additional challenges for keeping the rest of the room from getting wet when the shower is used.

One solution for this is to make the whole bathroom a wet room or shower room so that the entire space is capable of being wet.

It doesn't mean that you need to flood the bathroom or get everything in it soaked each time you take a shower. It just means that everything could get wet with no adverse effect — by intentional design.

Such a design further eliminates the need to consider keeping or adding glass partitions, shower doors, and even shower curtains.

It also allows the wet area of the shower (with one or more fixed showerheads or a handheld/personal shower) to be as large as necessary in the room without specifically defined boundaries.

This also facilitates using it effectively if you need to shower from a seated position on a bench or wheelchair, or if someone needs to assist you. It really adds flexibility to the bathroom.

Because all of the walls and floor are tiled, any water from the shower will drain to the primary or central floor drain.

The drain can be located under the showerhead or linearly from wall-to-wall (and parallel to the room's entrance door) along the general edge of the shower area.

The floor would need to be pitched correctly for proper drainage.

Pedestal sinks or wall mounted sinks may do well in such an application to save space and eliminate the need for cabinets.

Tankless and corner toilets can save some space also, but the soil pipe may need to be relocated.

Pocket doors or sliding doors may maximize the interior space without adding a door physically opening into the space — or out into the hallway.

Bath Temperature Setting/Scald Control

One way to avoid accidentally using water that is uncomfortably or dangerously hot in the bath or shower — and risking discomfort and possible injury — is by setting the hot water heater to a maximum temperature of 120°.

Most dishwashers and washing machines have the heating ability within them to create the temperature above this that they need to perform properly. So, a lower hot water temperature may be the solution for you and the others in your home — including visitors and houseguests.

Still, many people may prefer a hotter temperature for a shower or for washing dishes by hand. Just be careful with hotter water if you or others in your home have difficulty feeling hot temperatures in your hands or feet.

The safety and comfort solution here — and one regardless of ability or needs — is an easy-to-read digital temperature or scald control for the tub or shower.

It can be set for the desired temperature to keep the water from getting any hotter than what is selected.

Depending on how handy you are as the homeowner or renter, you can do this yourself — or you can have a handyman, kitchen and bath designer, plumber, or remodeler do it for you.

Folding Shower Seats

Some people need to sit down routinely in order to use the shower and bathe comfortably and effectively. If this is the case, they should have a seat installed or integrated into the shower design.

However, as a component of universal design, a folding seat is a good strategy that offers safety, comfort, accessibility, and convenience for everyone.

This way, the seat can be available when needed but stored against the rear or side shower wall and out-of-the-way when it isn't in use. This serves everyone.

In households where the seat is required all the time by one or more people, you can leave it fully deployed, or one can be built in.

For people who require it occasionally, however, the folding seat can be opened into the operational position, used, and then stored again against the wall when they are finished.

This can be installed for bathtub use as well.

Overnight or longer-term houseguests can take advantage of the folding seat also. It is intuitive and available to be deployed and used.

It can be designed in a variety of sizes and materials — as long as they are suitable for a wet area and can be cleaned easily. Also. they can be installed in all of the bathrooms rather than just the master.

Whether it's sitting to let the water massage a muscle pull or general muscles aches (or sore feet), sitting to keep stitches or surgical sites in the lower leg or foot from getting wet, sitting because of fatigue or low stamina, sitting to shave your legs, or sitting while someone assists with the bathing, a fold down seat accommodates a wide range of users and can be used when necessary and stored away when it isn't needed.

Because it needs to be anchored securely into the wall, and ceramic tile or other hard surface shower surround materials are involved, homeowners or renters may want to have a remodeler, handyman, kitchen and bath designer, or durable medical equipment specialist do this job.

If the walls have had wooden wall blocking installed during an earlier remodeling project or the original construction, this will facilitate the installation of the seat and allow more flexibility in choosing a location.

Boards that are installed edgewise between the studs and flush with the front surface of them is what is called "wall blocking." They allow items to be secured to them later on without needing to locate a stud or use wall fasteners or anchors.

Built-In Shower Seats

For those people who routinely need to sit down in order to use the shower and bathe comfortably, or those who would rather have a built-in seat instead of a fold-down version, choose a built-in seat that is integrated into the shower design. This can be formed into an acrylic or fiberglass shower base along with the shower pan, or it can be constructed and tiled as part of the shower.

The fold-down seat is a good universal design treatment for multiple users in a household or for people who don't need to use it every time they shower or bathe.

However, as a component of universal design, a permanently installed and built-in seat is also a good strategy for safety, comfort, and convenience — as long as it is designed and constructed well.

It needs to out-of-the-way so that it doesn't interfere with anyone entering and exiting the shower. It shouldn't be an impediment to passage or a potential tripping hazard. It should not infringe on open access or the passageway into the shower.

It needs to be high enough to safely sit on it but not so high that it is uncomfortable. If it is too low, there is a risk of falling while trying to sit on it.

Remember that it is going to be a tile surface so it will be hard and inflexible. Also. it needs to be designed so that it will drain well and not retain pooled water on it.

Make sure that it actually is built-in and tiled rather than just a wooden bench that is placed in the shower and not anchored.

While a wooden or plastic bench might make sense as far as moving it about in the shower or taking it out to clean it, it is unsafe because someone might trip on one of the legs, it might interfere with safely entering the shower, and it could tip if someone places their weight on it awkwardly. Keep this in mind when using or deciding on temporary transfer seats also.

If someone needs to transfer from a wheelchair to the built-in seat, make sure it is large enough and accessible enough to allow this — with grab bars as necessary.

Free-Standing Bathtubs

Many homes today are featuring free-standing bathtubs in the master bathroom — located in the middle of the floor with nothing around them, or near a wall but not attached to the wall.

These are not universal design features. They present many safety issues and generally are not desirable to have in your home.

They typically have tall sloping sides, and many are elevated from the floor on platforms, stands, or claw feet — making them even taller.

The risk of slipping getting in the tub — assuming your legs are long enough or you have sufficient flexibility in your hips and waist to climb over the edge of the tub — is high for anyone. Someone with poor balance, coordination, or range-of-motion — or someone who is short of stature — will find these tubs very hard to use.

They are aesthetically pleasing and add a decorator statement to a bathroom, but they are not functional for most people.

Since the tubs are located in the middle of the room (or sometimes next to a wall), there are no grabs bars or any other form of support to use in getting in or out of the tubs — nor on top of or inside the tubs. There are no steps to use getting into the tub.

These clearly are not a fixture you should have in your home as you are aging.

Additionally, they are relatively large and deep so they necessarily would hold a tremendous amount of water if they were to be filled — more than the volume of just one typical hot water heater.

Floor Mounted Plumbing

When free-standing bathtubs are used, they often have a water supply at the front or side of the tub that is exposed (rather than hidden or enclosed under the tub), and this creates a tripping hazard for anyone that might walk too closely to it or not realize that it is there.

By eliminating or choosing not to install the free-standing tub, this issue will not be a concern.

This is just another reason why these tubs are not a universal design product or practical for seniors.

Walk-In Bathtubs

At first glance these appear to be a great product for seniors as they offer independence and privacy for those desiring to bathe in a tub.

However, they are not a universal design product because they aren't practical for all ages to use — even though there is nothing technically preventing anyone from using it who can walk into it and sit down.

By their design and presence in a home, they say that someone needs special assistance bathing. Therefore, they are not universal design because they are noticeable as a special feature and are not unobtrusive.

The reason that walk-in tubs in master bathrooms seems to be a good idea for seniors is because it lets them bathe without assistance. Nevertheless, there are many potential drawbacks for including this feature.

First of all, this is not a do-it-yourself project. It will require professionals to install it and hook up all of the plumbing. The fixture itself can run several thousand dollars not counting installation, depending on which one is selected — and whether it has water jets or a heating feature.

There are many designs, styles, sizes, and shapes from which to choose.

Some are taller and narrower than others. Some are longer and a bit lower. Some fit in the space where a regular tub was. All take a very large volume of water to use them comfortably — more hot water than can be delivered by a typical gas or electric hot water tank unless a tankless hot water heater is added also.

Depending on the type of tub selected, the amount of water to fill it to a comfortable soaking level can be more than twice that of a standard bathtub.

Thus, as the tub is filling the water will begin to cool (unless there is a heating element in the tub), and your body will adjust to the water temperature so that it will seem cooler than it is.

The only way to add more hot water is to stand up (often without a grab bar to assist you to stand) and reach for the faucet. This poses many standing, slipping, sitting, and general comfort issues.

With any of the walk-in tubs, you must enter them and secure the door before you can turn on the water and adjust the temperature. Then you must sit there as the tub fills to the desired level.

You cannot open the door again until the water drains to below the bottom surface of the door. It generally takes a couple of minutes to drain the tub.

Some of the cabinets have locking latches that take a certain amount of strength and the ability to push down forcefully. This could be an issue for some people who aren't tall enough or lack sufficient range-of-motion or hand, arm, or shoulder strength..

Most of the models available have a very limited amount of grab bars integrated into their design. Typically there is one located inside the tub across from the door or on the back of the door, but almost none of them have a grab bar on the top edge or the outside of the tub near the door.

Should you begin to slip as you are exiting or entering the tub, there is no support and nothing to grab onto to prevent a fall.

Also many of the tubs have a fairly sizeable step up or down from the floor of the tub to the bathroom floor — plus a retaining lip to step over that the door closes against. This can be a safety issue.

There are many safety, comfort, and convenience issues associated with using a walk-in tub that seem to make them impractical for seniors. However, some people desire, want, and do use them.

Consider what each tub offers and then weigh any shortcomings or concerns before deciding which one to install or whether to have one at all. Then, if you do select one, make sure that it sized correctly for your needs and for the space where it is to be installed.

Soaking/Garden/Whirlpool Bathtubs

The soaking or garden tub (with or without whirlpool jets) was quite a popular feature in master bathroom designs for years, and builders offered them in new construction across a range of price points. Now the free-standing tub seems to have become just as popular, and I already discussed that on page 101.

You might have a garden, soaking, or whirlpool tub already, but as we age, range-of-motion, joint pain and stiffness, squatting, standing from a seated position, balance, coordination, and other concerns may affect us.

Many people find that stepping into and climbing from a soaking tub — without or without whirlpool jets or heat — can present many safety and comfort challenges. As a result, the tub sits there unused — occupying a very large part of the bathroom area.

Add to that the amount of water used to fill the tub, and the fact that the water tends to cool off quickly (to the extent that a heating element, if used, helps mitigate this) — these are issues that I mentioned for both the free standing tubs and the walk-in tubs also.

For seniors who are able to step into a traditional bathtub and use it safely, this is probably the best choice for taking a bath rather than the larger ones.

There is even a traditional tub that can be obtained or retro-fitted with a door into the wall of it — combining the access of a walk-in tub with the size and convenience or a regular tub.

Otherwise a shower with a seat is going to offer you what you need — especially when you have a handheld or personal shower wand that you can use.

Handheld/Personal Showers

The handheld or personal shower is a great universal design strategy that offers safety, comfort, and convenience for anyone.

It can be an auxiliary showering device to an existing fixed showerhead or the only showering fixture in a bathtub or stall shower. It may be mounted along a slide bar to rest on or in a holder or cradle, or it might retract into the tub fixture.

When the handheld or personal shower is mounted along a slide bar where it rests in a cradle attached to the slide bar, and the height of it can be adjusted up or down along the length of the bar, some people may choose to leave it in place at the selected height and just use it as a wall-mounted shower.

Others will remove the shower wand from the mount and hold it.

When a folding or stationary shower seat is used, the handheld shower — with sufficient hose length — can easily be used by someone while they remain seated. Make sure that a sufficiently long hose is installed for this purpose — and that it remains out of the way.

When bathing assistance is required — or when a particular skin area needs to remain dry — the handheld offers good flexibility.

The main safety concern with a handheld is the way it is mounted for storage on the wall. There are slide bars that are being manufactured as grab bars — even with small diameters — and these are great.

Make sure to look for such a slide bar with the ability to be used as a grab bar in an emergency because it will be used as such anyway — even if it's not designed or intended to be used that way — just because it is there.

In existing applications where a handheld shower already exists but with a slider or mount that is not designed to double as a grab bar, change it out with one that is designed for this purpose — and with stronger screws or anchors — so it can withstand a panic grab or offer additional support when needed.

Also, be careful that the hose attached to the personal shower wand is not a tripping hazard.

Adding a handheld shower can be a relatively simple do-it-yourself project, but a handyman or remodeler can do it as well.

Towel Bars/Hooks/Rings

This is a major safety concern in bathrooms.

Just as slide bars for a handheld or personal showers are not designed to be used as grab bars unless they are specifically manufactured and installed for this dual purpose of being a slide bar and a grab bar, towel bars generally are not designed to be used for support either.

Nevertheless, many towel bars and rings — especially those installed near or inside the tub or shower space — are used as a grab bar in a panic. When someone loses their balance and slips, they look for the first thing they can find to support their weight or break their fall. The towel bar looks like it will work.

Unfortunately, many towel bars will break when sufficient downward or gripping pressure is applied to them — such as during a panic fall — or they may pull lose from the wall.

They are only designed to support a few towels and not someone's full body weight or downward force as they are falling.

Even if the bars or rings don't actually break from the added pressure of someone trying to use them for support, they easily can pull lose from the wall.

Either way, they will fail to support someone — essentially because they are not designed for this emergency purpose. It is not a fault of the towel bars.

Nevertheless, there are towel bars specifically designed to be used as grab bars also.

The important safety consideration is that when a towel is on the bar or rod, someone may grab it rather than the bar, and the towel may slip off the bar and defeat the intended purpose. This issue is heightened when the towel bars are installed near the tub or shower.

For overall safety, comfort and convenience, towel bars should be mounted away from the actual shower or bath area so that they are not mistakenly or expediently used for support.

Use actual grab bars in and around your tub and shower areas.

Hooks for towels do not tend to keep the towels on them very well and can cause injury if someone falls against them — or slips or trips on the towel that has fallen to the floor.

Changing out towel bars or moving them generally can be handled by the homeowner or renter unless you don't feel comfortable undertaking a job such as this, it's part of a more comprehensive remodeling project that you are undertaking, or drilling through ceramic tile or marble is involved.

Remember that they need to be anchored well into the wall in order to be effective as a grab bar.

Strategic Grab Bars

People tend to associate grab bars in a residential setting with people requiring them due to age or a specific need.

However, they do serve a useful universal design function when used as a positive strategy, and anyone (regardless of age) can benefit from them.

I call this concept "strategic grab bars" because I think for safety, comfort, and convenience, a well-designed, well-located, and attractive grab bar should be positioned vertically near the entrance to every tub or shower — at a suitable height for use by everyone in the household.

I think that everyone at least once in their lifetime has needed a little extra support getting in or out of the tub or shower.

This could be because they slipped or lost their balance getting in or out of the tub or shower.

Perhaps they had an injury or recent surgery that kept them from putting their full weight on the ground, or they got a muscle cramp or spasm (in their leg, foot, or back) that interfered with their ability to stand or put their entire weight on their feet.

Maybe they were generally sore from exercise or other activity.

As we get older, our balance and coordination may not be as good as it was when we were younger.

So the strategic grab bar (or strategically placed grab bar, if you prefer) is a good universal design feature that can be incorporated into an aesthetically pleasing look. We can use it, regardless of our age or ability, and our houseguests will appreciate seeing it and being able to use it as they need it.

One grab bar is likely sufficient as a strategic grab bar. For functional grab bars, you will want to add at least one more.

"Pseudo" Grab Bars

Whether you are including a strategic grab bar on the wall at the back edge of a tub or shower (typically the one away from the shower head), or you are adding additional grab bars in the shower or bath area itself for additional safety and support, you will want to begin by looking for and removing all "pseudo-grab bars."

Replace anything that looks like you might grab onto it or reach for it for support when you slip — that really was never designed to function that way.

If they are located where you want them to be, then replace them with something that is specifically designed to provide the required support. Otherwise, just remove them and don't put anything in its place.

Towel bars, soap dishes, toothbrush holders, or anything similar in the bath or shower area that might be grabbed by someone in a panic situation (regardless of its size or shape) just are not designed to provide such support.

This would also include removing any grab bars mounted with suction cups. They simply cannot be relied upon to work when needed.

Grab bars must be designed to hold up to the pressure and force applied to them, and they must remain anchored to the wall.

They must be structurally sound and up to the task.

Because of the safety factor involved here, you want to make sure that all grab bars are installed properly, so a handyman, kitchen and bath designer, or remodeler may be the appropriate one to do it.

Functional Grab Bars

Strategic grab bars are universal. Everyone can use them, and they blend into any design without calling undue attention to them.

"Pseudo" grab bars are dangerous and need to be removed — or replaced with something more substantial that actually is created and designed to function as a grab bar.

That brings us to adding grab bars that can be installed as needed or desired for a specific purpose.

They won't be universal in the sense that they are totally unnoticeable, but in another way, they will roughly appear to be about the same as existing towel bars and other bathroom accessories that people have come to use as grab bars anyway in an emergency.

They also aren't universal in the sense that particularly young people will find them necessary or useful, but at a certain age everyone will appreciate having more than just the strategic grab bars at the entrance to the tub or shower — as long as they are designed and installed with function in mind rather than ADA compliance.

The two grab bars that typically are installed along the side wall and rear wall of a toilet location are totally impractical although they meet the national guidelines.

It takes more upper body strength (arms, shoulders, chest, and back) and joint health than most people possess to pull themselves from a seated position on the toilet (or their wheelchair) to a standing position — whether they are then transferring back to using a wheelchair or walker or not.

The bar behind the toilet serves no purpose at all in assisting someone to stand. The one on the side is roughly shoulder height when you are seated so it requires a lot of shoulder, chest, tricep, bicep, forearm, hand, and abdominal muscle strength (at a minimum) as well as good range-of-motion to be able to pull oneself into a standing position from a very awkward leverage standpoint.

So, make sure the functional grab bars — whether inside the tub or shower area or elsewhere in the bathroom — are strategically placed and at an appropriate height for you and others in your household to use them effectively.

Because residences are exempt from ADA requirements unless specifically demanded by your local building code, ignore the height recommendations and suggested locations. Go with a placement that makes sense for your and the ones in your home who will be using them.

One more thing about positioning the grab bars.

The strategic grab bars at the entrance to the tub or shower should be mounted vertically. The slide bars for the handheld showers also will be vertical.

Most of the other grab bars will be installed horizontally and parallel to the floor. There are "L" bars as well that are one piece vertical and horizontal bars.

There is a school of thought that likes to install grab bars on a diagonal with the thinking that this gives someone plenty of chances to grab the bar rather than locate it just in one position.

It appears, however, that in grabbing a diagonal device that you may very well slip along it and ride it to its lowest point. A vertical bar could do the same, but they tend to be shorter in overall length.

Therefore, a horizontally mounted bar (or "L" bar) is the best choice for supporting you at the point where it is grabbed.

Tilt-Out/Tip-Out Sink Front Bins

In the kitchen and baths (and occasionally in the laundry room), an area that goes unused that can be a great universal design strategy is the cabinet blank in front of the sink — one or two depending on the design, and with or without dummy drawer pulls.

For convenience and efficiency, these can be turned into functioning tilt-out or tip-out storage bins or trays — depending on their depth. Otherwise, they remain unused storage potential.

In the bath, they will replace medicine cabinets that tend to go unused as reaching for them becomes more of an issue as we age. The bins will bring handy, everyday grooming, hygiene, and other small useful items right to your fingertips.

People of any age or ability can use these as they require very little effort to pull them open, don't latch but stay in place with tension hinges, and don't have a particularly large capacity so weight is usually not a concern.

The main safety concern would be keeping sharp items (razor blades, scissors, sewing needles, syringes, and tweezers), medicines (prescription or over-the-counter), and other dangerous or unsuitable items from such bins if you are likely to have grandchildren living in your home or visiting you.

Depending on how complicated it is to get the blank cabinet fronts off and replace them with the bins, this could easily be a do-it-yourself project.

Certainly a handyman or remodeler could do it.

If you are replacing cabinets, look for ones where this design strategy can be employed.

There may not be enough room to use this technique with undermount or integrated bowl sinks because of the limited space between the cabinet and the edge of the sink bowl so check for available room first.

Body Dryer

This is very high-tech, modern, and state-of-the-art appliance — and it's a great universal design strategy.

It provides safety, comfort, convenience, and it is highly accessible.

This is a heated, forced air, electric dryer for use after showering. It is mounted in a corner of the shower and provides a series of heated air jets to blow dry anyone standing or seated in front of it much the same way that hair dryers or automatic hand dryers do.

They are said to take about the same amount of time that a person uses to towel dry, but towel drying does not remove all of the water like these do.

For anyone with range-of-motion issues, someone who might need help drying themselves, or anyone who needs to make sure they get completely dry, this is a great idea.

In addition to being functional, it's a great conversation starter when houseguests or friends see it. Plus, it is quite sanitary and saves on laundering towels.

This is specifically designed for use in a wet area and is hardwired into the electrical circuit. You may need an electrician, handyman, or remodeler to install it.

Toe-Kick Lighting

The toe kick — that little recess of a few inches tall by a few inches deep that keeps the base cabinets in the kitchen, bathroom, or laundry room from resting directly on the floor and gives people a place to put their feet to maintain their balance while in front of the cabinets — can be put to effective use with LED rope lighting, fluorescent strip lighting, xenon strip lighting, or LED strip lighting.

This provides additional indirect ambient lighting for any room where this lighting strategy is used — for safety or general illumination in an otherwise unused space.

It can be installed with a dimmer control if desired. It also can be switched, used with a timer or photo cell, or just left on because of its energy efficiency.

Depending on what type of lighting is selected and where the electrical outlet or electricity source happens to be, this might be as simple as plug-it-in-and-use it.

It might be an installation that you can do, or it might require the services of an electrician or low voltage electrical contractor (also called an electrical services contractor or "ESC").

It makes a great night or early morning light and helps out in low-light situations when overhead or other lights are not on or available.

Under-Cabinet/Task Lighting

The kitchen requires a variety of lighting sources since there are so many different types of tasks going on there. In addition to the toe-kick area, another underutilized area of the kitchen (and the bath and laundry room) for additional lighting is the area under the upper cabinets.

As is the case for toe-kick lighting, adding lighting under the cabinets might be a simple plug-in-and-use installation that you can do. It could require the services of an electrician or low voltage electrical contractor or electrical services contractor — depending on where the electrical outlet or electricity source happens to be and if a new connection or outlet has to be installed.

This could also be part of a larger kitchen (or bath) remodeling project.

This strategy and universal design treatment provides additional countertop, workspace, and indirect ambient lighting for the kitchen or bath.

It can be switched, used with a timer, or just left on because of its energy efficiency — LED rope lighting, fluorescent strip lighting, xenon strip lighting, or LED strip lighting.

This is a solution that provides additional safety and convenience by adding more light to the countertop work and prep surface and to the room in general. Just make sure that it doesn't create any glare on the countertop or small appliances.

This solution also makes a great night or anytime fill-in light and helps out in low-light situations when overhead or other lights are not switched on.

Overhead Lighting

At one time, homes were built with ceiling light fixtures in every room. You might be living in such a home currently.

While the centralized ceiling fixtures often delivered harsh, localized lighting that could cast strong shadows and didn't fill the entire room with effective lighting, each room at least had this light source.

For older homes where this is still true (where the ceiling fixtures haven't been removed or replaced with an updated one) and for newer homes where foyers, living rooms, dining rooms, bedrooms, kitchens, baths, hallways, stairways, laundry rooms, porches, patios, garages, closets, or basements may have ceiling light fixtures also, the light output is often insufficient for the activity in the room or space — making this a safety, convenience, and comfort issue.

Depending on the size, shape, design, and type of the ceiling lighting fixtures you have in your home, and the number and wattage of bulbs they can support, it may be possible to increase the light output to be more effective.

Just be aware that shadows and glare caused by brighter overhead lights may affect vision and depth perception and be a comfort and safety concern.

In some cases, increasing the bulb wattage may be sufficient to add more light to a room without casting unacceptable shadows, while in other instances a new or additional light fixture may be required as the solution.

As we age, we generally need more lighting to read and perform other tasks than we did when we were younger — lighting that is illuminating the page we are trying to read or the task we are working on rather than just general lighting of a space.

To supplement overhead lighting, you can use table lamps and floor lamps in bedrooms, living rooms, dining rooms, home offices, basements, porches, family rooms, and other living areas — again paying attention to the light output, shadows, glare, and "hot spots."

In living rooms, dining rooms, family rooms, bathrooms, and bedrooms, wall lamps or sconces offer supplemental lighting but generally not enough to light a large area.

In kitchens and bathrooms, the toe-kick and under-cabinet or task lighting that I mentioned are great supplemental lighting sources.

While consumers can change out light bulbs rather easily, you may or may not feel confident in replacing light fixtures and choose to rely on the services of a handyman, electrician, or remodeler. This would be especially true if a new receptacle, wall switch, or circuit needs to be installed or the fixture is particularly large or heavy.

Many ceiling fans come with light kits — optional or already installed. This provides a central ceiling lighting resource also — with the same issues as ceiling mounted fixtures in terms of light output, harsh light, glare, and shadows.

Light Bulb Choices

The type of light bulbs available for consumers to use in lamps, ceiling fixtures, and elsewhere around the home has changed rather dramatically in recent years.

Incandescent bulbs have been phased out. The CFL's (compact florescent bulbs) have safety, health, and practical concerns (they contain mercury and may not fit well or are unattractive) involved with using them.

Regular florescent tubes and rings (with less safety and health issues than CFL's but still some present) and halogen bulbs (although they produce a lot of heat and can cause a burn) can still be used.

However, LED lighting is the trend of the future. LED light bulbs tend to cost more initially but last several years, can be used with a dimmer, do not put out any appreciable heat, are being manufactured in higher wattage (what we normally think of as wattage) outputs, and are more widely available than they were.

The prices are dropping, and the market is getting quite competitive.

As we move to LED lights, we need to re-educate ourselves to choose the correct bulb. The traditional measurement of a bulb's brightness and light output for years has been wattage — 40w, 60w, 75w, and 100w, for instance.

Now, with the LED, we are more concerned with lumens (the amount or intensity of light produced) and color temperature (such as daylight, warm white, cool white) than with what particular wattage it is.

The LED does not produce as much light as an incandescent bulb of the same equivalency, but the lack of heat produced, the considerably lower energy consumption, and the length of time they last make LED's a much better choice than incandescent bulbs.

Ceiling Fans

Ceiling fans are great for providing comfort and air circulation. They can also function as ceiling light fixtures when the light kits are installed on them — as an optional feature or as part of the original package.

They can supplement other ceiling or wall-mounted light fixtures that you might have and can provide a central ceiling light for your room when none other exists (with one or more bulbs mounted in the center of the fan under the blade motor) or an array of several bulbs extending from the center. They come in a variety of styles and shapes also.

Keeping lights and fans dusted (for air quality and general appearance) and avoiding a strobing effect (to keep the fan from creating a pulsing light pattern on the walls, ceiling, floors, or furniture) are the main issues with ceiling fans and the lights attached to them.

For additional comfort and convenience, the fans can be regulated for speed (as well as downdraft or updraft) with a pull chain or a wall speed control switch, and the lights that are attached to them can be used with a dimmer control.

Some homeowners or tenants can install their own ceiling fans as long as they have the physical ability and range-of-motion to lift a somewhat heavy and awkward fan into position, maintain their balance, hold it in place while the wiring is connected, and attach it to the mounting hook or screws.

Otherwise, a handyman, electrician, carpenter, or remodeler can do this.

Skylights

Continuing the discussion of lighting in your home for comfort, safety, and convenience, let's look at skylights.

In any room where additional overhead lighting is desired — primarily during daylight hours — skylights are a good choice.

As long as they are installed properly so that there are no leaks, they are sized right for the space (a major universal design precept), and they are not shadowed excessively or blocked by overhanging tree branches (an occasional branch blowing in the breeze may be OK), skylights (when ceiling space and rafters accommodate or allow their use) can be an effective supplemental (and free) lighting source. They are sustainable and use no energy.

Also, they will reduce the energy demand for other lighting during daylight hours so there is an additional economic benefit as well. There is no direct cost to use them as a light source (after they are installed) and they save money by reducing the need for other lighting to be on.

Depending on how the rafters are configured relative to the ceiling in a particular room, the skylights may not be able to be as large as desired or centered in the room — aesthetics may be a factor in ultimately deciding on whether to use them in a specific room.

Skylights come in square and rectangular shapes with either flat or domed lenses — fixed and well as being able to be opened and closed with a motor.

They also come round with polished steel tubes connecting a ceiling lens or diffuser with the roof lens or collector (available in a variety of diameters and from various manufacturers).

The round skylights also have light kits so that they can double as a ceiling light during evening hours or other times when supplemental room lighting is needed.

This project definitely will require the services of a remodeler, carpenter, handyman, roofer, or skylight installer — and possibly an interior designer, architect, and electrician (for the light kit) — to make sure the skylights are located correctly, the roof and ceiling are cut in the right place, the alignment is made with the ceiling location, everything is trimmed out properly, and that there are no leaks.

Eye-Level Controls

This is a universal design element that addresses accessibility, comfort, convenience, and safety issues in your home.

Often the wall-mounted controls in a home, such as thermostats and switches for ceiling fans (and even some light switches) are mounted higher than eye level (making them hard to see and use easily) or beyond the easy reach of your grandchild, a short adult, or a person in a wheelchair.

However, regular light switches typically are located at a reasonable height.

Controls in any room that are located generally less than 48" (4 feet) above the floor surface allow the widest range of accessibility and usage.

Thus, by lowering the switches and controls, a small adult (or grandchild), those who might be in a wheelchair, those who might have physical limitations that keep them from standing erect (including those requiring support from a cane or walker), and those with range-of-motion issues in their elbows or shoulders that prevent a normal arm extension could reach them — in addition to those of average or above average height who could reach something mounted higher.

Sometimes mixing or distribution valves in tubs and showers, the digital displays and controls for wall ovens and microwaves, and exhaust fan switches and work lights on range hoods fall into this same category of being mounted higher than easily accessible or visible in terms of being able to use them easily.

Eye level for a typical adult in a wheelchair is defined by the ADA as 51" — a smaller or larger person could experience a little variation in this number.

Therefore, keeping all controls and switches no higher than 48" from the floor is a good design practice.

If wall controls are placed in the general vicinity of light switches, they would be more convenient and aesthetically pleasing than having them take up more wall space and not be as centrally located on your wall.

In terms of safety and comfort, it's beneficial for more rather than fewer people in the home to be able to access and use these controls — including being able to read them and set them (such as thermostats) because they are at a comfortable height.

If the wiring going to the controllers or devices is long enough to allow relocating or moving them without any rewiring, this could be a do-it-yourself project for you.

Of course, the walls would need to be patched and repainted where the former installations were.

An electrician, handyman, or remodeler may need to do this work — especially if there is not enough wire going to the controller or switch to allow it to be moved without running more wiring or you don't feel comfortable with working around electrical wires.

Electrical Outlets

Depending on the building codes in effect where you are, the standard location of an electrical outlet from the floor is likely fine — as long as it's not in the floor.

However, installing standard electrical receptacles higher than usual above the floor so they are in easy reach of everyone is a good universal design strategy as long as they are not so high as to call attention to their placement by looking unusual.

In some rooms such as kitchens, bathrooms, and laundry rooms, the outlets tend to be higher anyway — just over the height of countertops or adjacent to them.

Sometimes, they are mounted in the sides of the base cabinets if they are accessible in the room.

In other rooms such as bedrooms, outlets can be a little higher because furniture often hides them and makes them difficult to access when installed closer to the floor.

The height from the floor that outlets normally are placed is not inconsistent with the ADA guidelines (9" for direct access by a person in a wheelchair and 18" for someone reaching out for it from a wheelchair position), but if they were installed a little higher, more people could reach them easier without bending so much.

This would include taller adults, people using a walker, people with range-of-motion issues, and those who have difficulty bending down or standing up again.

Depending on how many outlets need to be moved and how sufficient the wiring is going to the various outlets, this could be a do-it-yourself project. Attic or basement access might be necessary as well.

The walls would need to be patched and repainted where the former boxes were.

An electrician, handyman, or remodeler may need to do this work — especially when there is not enough wiring to move the boxes without running more wiring.

Wall-Mounted Mirrors

All homes need mirrors, and they are generally found in bathrooms, bedrooms, and foyers or hallways.

Many are decorative mirrors — regardless of their size or shape — that are framed and hung on the wall like a picture.

Some, such as in bathrooms, are large and mounted directly to the wall with adhesive or clips.

Others are considered to be "full-length" and attached to the back of a door.

Still others are used as bypass or bi-fold closet door panels.

The way that mirrors become a universal design concept and strategy is when they are accessible and usable by everyone in the home.

They don't necessarily have to be a tilted mirror that adjusts on a pivot (aiming somewhat downward with the top of the mirror being further from the wall than the bottom), but this can be a universal design treatment if everyone in the home can use the mirror comfortably and see themselves in it.

Generally, the height at which tilting or fixed mirrors are mounted and the focal length created by the installation (particularly with a tilted mirror) means that the mirrors are too high to see more than just your head and upper torso.

Mirrors mounted behind the sink are generally no lower than 30" unless the countertop is lower. Often mirrors are higher than this because of a clearance space allowed between the countertop and the bottom of the mirror.

This is true even when there is a sit-down vanity.

Additionally, there usually there is a wall opposite the wall-mounted mirror that keeps someone from backing up far enough to get a longer vertical view and see themselves effectively.

Even when you get a full body view from a wall-mounted mirror, the distance is such that you are quite far from the mirror. Then, being able to see much detail for grooming or choosing an outfit becomes an issue.

Lighting above or around the mirrors further affects the functionality of the mirrors due to glare, "hot spots," insufficient lighting, shadows, and the color temperature of the bulbs.

Full-length and closet door panels offer a much better solution than wall-mounted mirrors because they accommodate any physical size.

A toddler, a person in a wheel chair, and a basketball player can all see themselves in such mirrors. You can get as close as necessary to the mirror.

In selecting mirrors, pay attention to the weight of the mirrors relative to where they will be installed or used, how you intend to mount them, the likelihood of the mirrors beginning to de-silver along the edges, and the general quality of the glass so imperfections are avoided. Nevertheless, mirrors are relatively inexpensive to purchase.

Some homeowners and renters can handle a project of this nature (especially if someone else can help you hold and support part of the mirror while you are installing it), but a professional can do this easily.

Visual Indicators

I have already talked about visual clues to indicate relative temperatures and to show where light switches and other controls are located.

Additionally, there are other visual indicators that are universal design concepts that are effective.

For the hearing impaired, doorbells and telephones are often connected to one or more lights throughout the home that flash when someone rings the doorbell or calls on the phone.

They might be in the living room, kitchen, bedroom, or other areas of the home.

They are a great feature for anyone (and thus universal in concept) because they provide another — and silent — way of alerting us to the presence of someone at the front door or on the phone (for those people who have a landline).

With all of the noise present in a home from time-to-time — from TVs, music players, computer videos, conversation, appliances, vacuum cleaners, fans, air conditioners, and other devices — having a visual way of knowing when someone is at the door or calling on the phone would help everyone.

There are traffic, airplane, machinery (such as lawn mowers), and other outside noises present at various times also.

Small children such as your grandchildren could easily see and recognize the visual signal, as could anyone else in the home.

This is a feature that offers safety, comfort, and convenience to the home and its occupants.

There are some easy-to-install kits that can be obtained from electronic stores for you to install yourself.

Otherwise, an electrician, handyman, ESC (low-voltage electrical services contractor), or remodeler can do this job for you.

5

Other Universal Design Safety & Convenience Strategies

More Universal Design Strategies For Safety, Convenience, Comfort And Accessibility

There are several other universal design strategies, treatments, and recommendations that we should look at that positively impact the overall quality of life in your home.

Many design concepts and solutions can be used as part of a more comprehensive remodeling than just changing out a few fixtures or moving the location of various controls.

The objective with such design considerations is increasing the comfort, safety, convenience, and accessibility for your general well-being (and the others in your household) as you remain living in your home.

Some of these concepts are going to have wider appeal and interest than others, but all can be effective. Most of them are true universal design, and the others will appeal more to seniors.

These strategies will require some advance planning and consultation. In some cases, major changes are involved.

The issue is not whether they are good design or will make your home safer and more comfortable but whether you want to incorporate them in any renovation projects that you are doing or planning.

Budget and time to complete them are certainly considerations in deciding which projects to undertake.

Contrast And Glare

As we age, we need more light to read and to see objects close up that we want to examine. We have already looked at this.

At the same time, however, our eyes are more affected by bright lights and glare. We are more susceptible to misjudging distances and determining how close objects are that might be in front of us.

Some people have more pronounced vision issues than others — regardless of age.

There are vision issues that many people deal with as they age including cataracts, glaucoma, and macular degeneration.

Astigmatism also affects many people throughout their lifetime and the way glare impacts them. It tends to be more prevalent with aging.

Therefore, two strategies that are effective for eliminating glare or confusion about surfaces and where objects are located are the use of color or contrast and using less shiny or reflective surfaces.

I already mentioned color with respect to hot and cold running tap water and the use of visual indicators.

Glass (window glass, mirrors, glass panels in appliances, glass top tables (coffee tables, end tables, and breakfast or dinette tables) and glass shower enclosures — if you haven't removed them yet) as well as hard surfaces such as countertops, appliance fronts (unless they have a matte finish), and ceramic and polished hardwood flooring are especially prone to reflecting light sources and creating glare when overhead lights are used. Sometimes natural light can do this also.

Shiny or foil wallpaper in bathrooms or laundry rooms can create "hot spots" from lights in those rooms or the way sunlight reflects off them. Glossy walls and other painted surfaces can do this as well.

Sometimes it's not the sheen but the busyness of the pattern that creates the issue. Certain wallpaper, mosaic floor or wall tile, or patterned artwork can impact orientation and affect balance if it has a particularly repetitive or busy pattern.

In kitchens, people often select a monochromatic look to create an aesthetically pleasing appearance — where the cabinets, flooring, and appliances all have a similar color, hue, or finish — but this is not the best design for universal accessibility, safety, and comfortable use.

It needs to be obvious where countertops and floors are located and not just have them blend from one surface to another.

A technique for defining countertops is something called "edge-banding" where a contrasting color is used on the edge of the countertops to show where the countertop surface begins. Doing this with some hard surfaces such as granite or quartz will take more effort and will add to the cost, but it will make the kitchen safer.

Just having the countertop edges or surface be a different color while everything else in the room is a similar color or hue will not be enough to add a safe amount of contrast. Your eyes must be able to distinguish various surfaces and features in the room.

This is commonly a kitchen issue but can be found in bathrooms, bedrooms, and laundry rooms also.

As for the flooring, toe-kick lighting that I already mentioned will illuminate part of the floor to show its location relative to the cabinets and reduce glare as well.

Using red knobs on stove or cooktop fronts is a similar strategy.

Listello

Listello is a border tile or pattern (although it can be wallpaper or other materials that serve the same purpose).

Normally it is used in ceramic or glass tile backsplashes or shower surrounds (as a smaller or contrasting tile and color) as a way of breaking up the large expanse of tile and adding visual interest. It gives our eyes something on which to focus.

It helps with reducing glare and improving orientation.

It can also be used on flooring — tile (ceramic, porcelain, or vinyl) or hardwood (parquet or a different stain color) — to break up a long run of flooring or to differentiate spaces in the home where no doorways or walls exist, such as from the living room to the dining area, or from the foyer or hallway to the living room, kitchen, or family room.

The important thing to keep in mind for using listello on walls is that it needs to be at eye level or a little below. If it's too high, it is ineffective and looks out-of-place.

Using the general guideline of 48" for the general maximum height that applies to all of the switches and controls in your home would be a good start — raising or lowering it somewhat from that point to look appropriate for the space and for the average height of those in your home.

Flooring

Flooring is a matter of personal choice, but there are types of flooring that tend to be more problematic than others for air quality, maintenance, sustainability, accessibility, comfort, and safety.

Thus, there are universal design choices and strategies concerning flooring. In general, carpeting is not a good choice anywhere in your home.

Carpeting was once quite popular, and many homebuilders still include it, but when it gets wet from rain or snow being tracked onto it, or from outerwear, shoes, or umbrellas dripping onto it — or when the door is opened and the wind blows in the rain or snow — it tends to remain wet for a period of time. Pets will track in the precipitation and dirt also.

Wet carpeting is more susceptible to attracting dirt — leaving noticeable dirty marks or stains that remain even after the area is dry.

Carpeting shows stains from food (especially ones with sauces, condiments, and gravies) and beverage spills (wine, fruit juice, Kool-Aid, coffee, tea, milk). It stains from pet accidents, blood from cuts, and anything else tracked or spilled onto it (oil, grease, mud).

Carpeting tends to off-gas, and it retains dirt and other pet and airborne allergens. More than other types of flooring, it develops noticeable wear patterns.

It presents air quality issues and typically needs replacing every few years. It also fades from the UV rays in sunlight and florescent lighting.

Carpeting needs constant vacuuming, steam cleaning, or shampooing to help it retain its look, but it is never really showroom clean again. Small, sometimes sharp objects (even hard or sharp plant material or seeds) can fall into the carpet and be unnoticeable until stepped on.

Hard surface flooring is the best to use, but hardwood flooring or hardwood-like flooring (engineered wood, laminates, and bamboo) should not be used in wet areas. Moisture causes the grain to expand and contract and affects the seams and joints.

Laminates and engineered wood flooring do not breathe, so any water or liquid spilled on them will be trapped beneath them when it seeps through the joints and seams.

Bamboo is water resistant (not waterproof), but it is not recommended for use in areas where it could get wet.

Ceramic tile — especially the new reticulated tile that fits together tightly and requires very small to even no grout joints — is a hard surface that holds up well to water, spills, and foot traffic. This reduces difficulties in getting wheels to travel over grout lines.

Tile is available in a variety of sizes and colors to match the color palette of the room in which it is installed and fit the proportions of the room.

The main issue with ceramic flooring is safety — it can be slick or slippery when wet, shiny to the point of creating glare (as I already mentioned), and hard to get good traction for walking across safely or using an aid such as a cane or walker.

In these cases, treads of some type or a smaller tile or mosaic pattern that is inlaid in places will provide more traction.

Ceramic tile typically shows wear patterns less than other types of flooring.

For years, vinyl flooring was not that popular except for relatively small applications (kitchens, laundry areas, mud rooms, foyers, and secondary bathrooms), but it has made a comeback.

It generally is well accepted and comes in a variety of sizes, styles (some look like ceramic tile or wooden planking), patterns and colors. It offers some cushion so it is easier on the feet and legs when standing on it and comes in several sizes and installation options.

Another type of flooring material that seems to work well — especially in the kitchen — is the natural product cork.

Cork is especially nice to stand on and helps to cushion dishes and glasses when they are accidentally dropped onto it. However, it does need to be sealed to guard against water penetration and stains.

Some homeowners will be able to accomplish flooring removal and replacement, but most will rely on handymen, flooring contractors, tile setters, or remodelers. It also depends on what is being removed as far as dust and debris.

There also is the issue of disposing of the removed product.

If you are removing tile that has been in place for years, approach it cautiously. It could have asbestos in the tile or in the mastic used to adhere it to the floor.

If you suspect this is the case or you are unsure, have it evaluated before proceeding.

Area Rugs

While aesthetically beneficial, area rugs are similar to carpeting in several respects and can be a slipping or tripping hazard — particularly when used in doorways between rooms or in the kitchen or bathroom in front of the sink.

Nearly everyone is susceptible to this danger, but vision difficulties may cause this to be more of an issue.

Like carpeting, area rugs hold dirt and allergens. They generally can be laundered more frequently than carpeting and often can be washed in your automatic washing machine (depending on size). They can be heavy and awkward to handle, however (especially when they are wet).

To maintain true universal design, the use of area rugs and carpeting in the home would be disallowed for safety, air quality, maintenance, general comfort, and accessibility.

They often get in the way of opening doors or moving carts, wheelchairs, or walkers across the floor.

Automatic Dustpan

Keeping hard surface floors clean requires constant attention. Vacuuming or sweeping with a broom are daily activities to keep the floors presentable.

There are vacuums, electric brooms, and other devices that can be used, but they tend to be a little bulky, can be hard for some people to move them about, and generally require electricity to use them.

There are manual mops, brooms, and sweepers, but a device that is universal that may have application for you is the automatic dustpan.

A central vacuum system is required for this feature to work so a remodeling contractor or a central vacuum installer may be needed to accomplish this design.

You also need the space to install it.

Do-it-yourselfers can complete this project, depending on how easy it is to gain access to the walls and attic or basement and how much disruption in the home can be tolerated while it is being installed. Some drywall repair and painting likely will be required.

A central vacuum system is a great idea to have in the home, but it is not purely a universal design feature.

It offers convenience as far as being able to plug the hose into various wall ports located around the home instead of moving an upright or canister vacuum cleaner around the house, but it still requires some physical size, strength, range-of-motion, stamina, and coordination to be able to use it effectively.

The automatic dustpan port is a station connected to the central vacuum that is installed at floor level in the baseboard (available in various finished and colors).

It is activated by a foot switch.

Simply sweep the floor and move the dust pile to the automatic dustpan where it can be vacuumed away into the holding tank.

This is a universal design feature because anyone capable of using a broom — even from a wheelchair or while using a walker — can sweep a pile of dust toward the automatic dustpan.

The switch on the port can be activated without bending down. Just step on it or use the broom handle or similar object to activate it.

This also is another way to improve indoor air quality by making it easier to remove dust from the floors.

Of course, you or someone else in your home will need to be able to empty the vacuum tank occasionally.

Room-To-Room Transitions

When two different types or thicknesses of flooring meet in a doorway — or between rooms even without an actual doorway — an uneven transition between the two surface results, and it can present comfort, safety, and accessibility issues.

The same can be true for decks, porches, and stoops outside or at the entrance to your home.

Even using a molding strip (metal, wood, rubber, or vinyl) between the two surfaces, going from one surface height (regardless of what it is) to another can present challenges for young grandkids pushing toys along the floor, baby strollers, walkers, wheelchairs, and even furniture or carts on casters.

Walking from one surface to the other — whether someone is using a cane or walker or not — can even be a potential tripping or stumbling hazard for anyone who puts their weight down awkwardly on the higher or lower surface and twists their ankle or loses their balance.

Perhaps they might catch the heel of their shoe or their toe (wearing shoes or not) on the molding and then stumble or lose their balance.

A uniform thickness of flooring — even if it's not the same product throughout the home — is the safe and comfortable way to handle this issue.

Depending on the number of instances where this exists in your home, it might be a do-it-yourself project to remedy the affected areas.

More than likely, this type of project will need to be done by a remodeler or flooring contractor.

Of course, replacing or redoing the flooring in most or all of your home will eliminate this issue. This would be a great opportunity to eliminate carpeting and solve the additional issue of uneven transitions at the same time.

For transitions between indoor and outdoor spaces, look for ways to make the transition smooth with the smallest difference possible. Ideally the space can be ramped or otherwise made smooth so that an actual step up or down isn't necessary — even if there is no easy way to change the levels between the two surfaces.

Chair Rail

Chair rail or chair railing is a decorative molding that many people use in certain areas of their home (such as the dining room or hallway) or even throughout the entire home as an accent.

However, it can have a universal design application that will allow anyone who needs a little extra support to use it without it being a feature that calls attention to itself.

When someone enters a home and sees wooden or metal grab bars lining the hallway or other areas of the home because one of the occupants of that home needs them for support (in addition to or in place or a walker, cane, or other mobility assistance), it is obvious that this is a specialized installation as opposed to a universal design that is applicable to everyone.

Nevertheless, such a feature can be accomplished as a universal design.

Chair rail, when it is used, is generally installed about one-third of the distance up from the floor to the ceiling or some 32"-36" with an 8' ceiling. It can be a little lower or a little higher, but this range falls in line with ADA guidelines for the height of a grab bar anyway.

Chair rail is available in many different profiles, designs, and dimensions plus ones that can be created by combining two or more stock designs, and it typically is installed parallel to the floor and flush against the wall surface.

However, for use as an unobtrusive grab bar, install the chair rail as a small board on the wall (1" x 3", 1" x 4", or 1" x 6") with a larger board attached directly to it.

This outer board can either be a 1" board (typically only ¾" thick although it is called a 1" board although truly 1" lumber — called "five-quarter" or 5/4 — can be obtained and used for a little extra spacing between the outer board and the wall).

Then the outer board of either a 1" (actually ¾") or 2" (really 1½") thickness board (that is wider than the board attached to the wall) should be attached directly to the board that is touching the wall.

The outside board can have additional molding attached to it to make it look more decorative if you like, but it should have the top of it rounded (called "bull nose").

It can be painted a complementary color for the walls in that room, or it can be stained. Be sure to test fit it before installing it to determine that the person you are creating it for can grasp the railing and that their fingers will fit in the space between the inner and outer boards.

Adjustable Shelving

Sometimes the height differential between members in a household is so great that solutions are sought for accommodating the location of shelving or countertops (all, some, or just a portion) in closets, kitchens, and other areas where people can access them easily.

Even when shelves and countertops are installed at conventional heights, some people find that this is too high while others need them even higher. Of course, many people are fine with the typical installation.

For homes where there is a desire to accommodate this height differential or otherwise provide a higher or lower cabinet or closet shelf, or part of a countertop, for those using assistance such as a wheelchair, or to allow people to sit when preparing meals or grooming because of personal preference, stamina, circulation, or balance issues, a solution lies in adjustable shelving.

There are two ways to accomplish these adjustments: motorize them or create a manual solution.

The motorized approach may be more than you want to budget, but it works for anyone in your home. Simply push the controller to raise or lower a shelf or countertop, and it will move up or down to the desired position. When the person who moved it is finished, it can be returned to its normal position or allowed to remain where it is until the next time it is needed.

With the manual approach, this will take someone with the physical ability and strength (and range-of-motion) to reach and grasp the handle of the pull-down (above them or in front of them) or pull-up shelf or countertop unit (located at waist level or below them) and leverage it up or down into the desired position.

For this to work well, choose a shelving unit with gas pistons that assist and minimize the effort needed to operate it. They will also stabilize the movement so you don't lose control. Older style adjustable shelving systems have stiff tension springs that are much harder to operate and control.

This feature will work in a closet to move items around on a track or bring a shelf to within reach for convenience or accessibility.

It can be used in the bath or powder room to move a sink (vessel or one mounted in a small countertop) up and down as long as the water supply lines and drain tubing are flexible and installed with this in mind.

It can be used in the kitchen to provide comfortable and accessible eating space by moving a countertop section up or down. It also can be used to raise or lower cabinets, shelving, cooktops, and sinks.

A handyman, kitchen and bath designer, interior designer, remodeler, or electrician would be a good resource for accomplishing this — depending on the extent of the changes desired.

Only for someone very experienced in do-it-yourself electrical and mechanical projects might this be done by the owner or tenant.

Kitchen Islands

In homes where there is an island as a feature in the kitchen, a couple of safety, convenience, and access issues need to be addressed.

Most of the islands I have seen are too large for the kitchen floor space so your island (if you have one) may need to be reduced in size.

People like the idea of having an island, but quite often there simply is not enough space around the island for two people to be in the same area at the same time, or for a cabinet or appliance door to open easily. Sometimes it's difficult for even one person to navigate the space around the island.

There needs to sufficient clear space — generally 48"-60" (four-five feet) — around each of the three or four sides of the island where cabinets, appliances, tables, passageways, or other functional areas of the kitchen are located.

It's not just a matter of someone in a wheelchair or walker being able to move around the island easily — although that certainly is a concern.

This is a matter of general access and function as well as comfort, convenience, and safety.

While wheelchair access is a consideration, it's a larger issue of two or more people — comfortably and safely — being able to be in the kitchen at the same time without bumping into each other, blocking the passageway, or interfering with what the other one is doing.

This would be true whether they are standing or seated. Even if you live alone, there may be times that you have family or guests visiting.

Sometimes when the islands are really large for the kitchen space, it's tight for even one person to be in the kitchen and move around comfortably.

Actions such as opening and using the microwave, opening cabinet doors and drawers, using the oven or cooktop, opening the dishwasher, and opening the refrigerator (or getting water or ice from the in-door dispenser) could be challenging.

When two or more people are in the kitchen together or at the same time — even for different reasons or purposes — any number of actions, including meal preparation or work at the sink could be happening.

Regardless of the size of the island — after it is adjusted to fall within acceptable clearance distances — all of the corners should be rounded with a radius sufficient to prevent injury from accidentally bumping into it while walking past or falling against it.

For universal design, if the resulting island is large enough for someone to sit down at it and eat — rather than just being a food preparation area or serving station — part of the countertop should be low enough and open enough to allow people to sit at it (or pull up a wheelchair) and eat.

In such cases, remember to mark the edges of the countertop to show that they are at different heights.

Restyling or resizing an island will likely involve the services of a handyman, kitchen and bath designer, interior designer, cabinet installer, remodeler, carpenter, electrician, or plumber — or several of them — depending on the extent of the changes needed.

A consumer experienced with do-it-yourself projects of this magnitude might be able to tackle this.

Be careful not to use a rolling table as a substitute for an island. While it might be small enough to fit within the space guidelines, it presents additional challenges by possibly moving while someone is using it and with where it is stored when not in use.

Modular Sink Base Cabinets

While having roll-in access to the kitchen or bathroom sinks is often desired, not everyone needs it. For this reason, it's not recommended as a universal design feature.

Nevertheless, as both a universal design and adaptable design feature, sink base cabinets in the kitchen and bathrooms can be designed and created intentionally to be removed later on as necessary — to create a more open look or to allow wheelchair access.

When the sink base cabinet is designed and created as a modular unit, it can be taken out (with those cabinets on either side of it remaining in place) to allow full access for someone in a wheelchair or just more open space for use with a chair or bench.

The removable, modular sink base cabinet would be a unit entirely separate from the rest of the cabinetry that can be installed along with the cabinets on either side of it but removed later without affecting the integrity of the remaining cabinets or countertop.

It is universal because it shows no outward sign of being any different from the other cabinets at present, but it is easily adaptable when the time comes for a fully accessible sink by simply pulling the modular sink base unit out and removing it.

There are other solutions for creating wheelchair access at the sink by removing the cabinet doors and cabinet floor or designing them to be retracted. Also, the height of the countertop might need to be adjusted to make sure that it can be accessed effectively.

If you need wheelchair access at the sink now — in either the kitchen or bath, or both — go ahead and create the specific design for it.

If it is a future possibility or you just want to be ready for this should it be necessary, the modular sink base is a good feature to use.

Again, a wall hung sink or a pedestal sink would allow wheelchair access without any other design changes required or necessary.

If it's just installing modular cabinets and securing them, a homeowner experienced in this type of job might do it. For the countertop, plumbing, and other aspects of this project, a remodeler, carpenter, plumber, electrician, or kitchen and bath designer may be needed.

Retractable Sink Base Cabinet Doors

While a modular sink base cabinet can be installed to be removed at a later date to provide wheelchair or open access to a sink, a universal design solution rather than an adaptable one is to create retractable doors on the sink base cabinet.

To allow access whenever someone needs to roll up to the sink from a wheelchair — or use it from a seated position (for stamina or just convenience) — the doors on the cabinet can be created to retract on a track or groove along the inside walls or ceiling of the cabinet much like the doors on a TV cabinet or entertainment center used to do.

It may not even be necessary to remove the toe-kick, but if that is desired, there are two way to handle this.

The toe-kick (the part of the cabinet floor extending from the door to the vertical toe-kick riser as well as the riser itself) for this base cabinet can be removed and left off so that when the doors are opened and used in the retracted position, the place where the toe-kick normally is would be empty.

The cabinet floor also can be hinged and lifted up and raised back inside the cabinet (with the toe kick riser either coming with the floor or remaining in place). If it moves with the cabinet flooring, the toe-kick can be moved out of the way when cabinet access is desired even if the doors are just opened and not retracted.

With this method, the outward appearance is the same whether or not the cabinet is designed for wheelchair access — instead of having a noticeable missing toe-kick.

Another solution is to remove the toe-kick and then to reconfigure the remaining cabinet floor.

It can be designed as an plumbing access panel (when access is to the water supply pipes or trap is needed or desired) on a slant to provide open floor space in front of it, conceal the plumbing behind it, and have narrow open shelves on it for storing cleaning products and paper goods.

The doors need to be kept from moving inward past the flush closed position when not retracted. A stop, pin, cleat, or other device needs to be used to achieve this.

A homeowner experienced in woodworking type projects might be able to do this; however, a remodeler, carpenter, cabinet installer, or kitchen and bath designer may be needed.

Cabinets And Drawers

Cabinets (and closets) are a big focus of universal design because they are used in many rooms throughout the home, and storage is something everyone needs.

There are several other universal design strategies and treatments involving upper and base cabinets — beyond what I already mentioned about the pulls, the tilt-out/tip-out bins, the lighting, the modifications to the sink base cabinets, and the adjustable shelving or tops.

There really are two main issues concerning cabinets: accessibility and ease of use.

In designing cabinets for replacement or in reworking existing cabinets — in the kitchen, bathrooms, basement, laundry room, linen closet, bedroom closets, garage, summer kitchen, mud room, patio, home office, dining room, hallways, or anywhere else they are located in the home — look at the size of the doors and drawers, the physical weight of the doors and drawers, the flexibility of using the storage space, the location of the door or drawer pulls on the actual doors or drawers, and the amount of room in front of them for someone to access them.

Ease of retrieving items that are stored is a big, and very important, issue. With drawers or pull-out shelves, bins, or baskets, the suspension system needs to provide sufficient support for the weight and easy movement of the drawers, shelves, bins, or baskets in and out — whether they are empty or loaded to capacity.

Thus, they should not be dependent on someone of any particular strength or ability being able to use them, and they should work equally well whether they are being accessed by someone from a standing, seated (such as on a chair, stool, or bench or from a wheelchair), or kneeling position.

To appeal to everyone in the household — regardless of their age, size, or ability — a good design idea for ultimate storage efficiency is to approach it much the same way that we want the controls to be located in the home (roughly 48" or less from the floor).

Obviously, cabinets are taller than that and can go all the way to the ceiling, but they should be designed so that most of the commonly used items are easily accessible and retrievable at eye level or below.

Keeping the items most in demand and most frequently used at least one shelf up from the floor is part of this same strategy — to reduce the need for bending and straightening up again.

Another strategy is to install upper cabinets actually resting on the countertop. While this concept makes them more accessible, it takes away useable counterspace that must be accounted for and accommodated elsewhere in the room.

An island — if the dimensions of the kitchen and intended size of the island permit it to be used — can be a solution.

An alternative is to mount one or more upper cabinets lower than their traditional height but still up from the countertop a few inches — making them easier to reach than at their traditional height and preserving some countertop functionality.

Another good idea is to look for smaller doors and cabinets so that a floor-to-ceiling linen, pantry, or supply cabinet can actually have two or more separate parts rather than a very tall closet-like cabinet — that comes with a necessarily heavier, larger, and harder-to-control door.

Some designers and consumers are returning to an open-look where just open wall shelves are used for storing or displaying cups, glasses, and dishware — in place of actual cabinets. There may or may not be upper cabinets used in conjunction with this design.

The openness certainly enhances accessibility; however, safety may be more of a concern as objects could fall or be knocked from the shelves.

Along this same line, open cabinets are being used that have no doors on them. Again, access is enhanced, but items knocked out or falling from the cabinet may present safety concerns. Also, keeping the dishware and glasses dusted is necessary since there are no doors to protect them. Clutter is another potential issue with open shelves.

Another concept that designers are using is to have all-drawer units in the base cabinets instead of doors that open with traditional shelving inside the cabinet. These allow you to organize and find like items in a drawer rather than bending down or reaching to access a shelf.

There are even corner drawer base units where the drawer fronts come together to form an interior 90° corner and the drawer comes out of the corner at a 45° angle. This brings items to the front and eliminates the blind corner or the need for a Lazy Susan for those not fond of this device.

Still, the drawers need to have a good suspension system that allows them to glide open and the close easily. Otherwise, the doors will work better — especially if hand or arm strength is an issue or concern.

Also, the drawers — depending on their depth and the extent to which they are opened — could require more access room around them than opening a cabinet door.

Depending your ability and expertise, you may be able to do some or all of the work on the cabinets; however, the services of someone such as a handyman, remodeler, carpenter, kitchen and bath designer, architect, interior designer, or occupational therapist may be beneficial for an effective design and proper installation.

Countertop Heights

There are commonly accepted standards for countertop height, but they can be raised or lowered to make your life more comfortable and convenient.

There really isn't a good universal design standard for countertop height because one low enough to serve children and short adults would be too low for taller individuals, and countertops designed for taller people would be difficult for shorter people to use. That's why the adjustable countertop could be a good solution.

Additional considerations comes into play as we age.

People with bad backs who can't bend at the waist very well might like a countertop higher than the traditional 36" kitchen counter or 29"-30" bathroom heights. In fact, a 36" bathroom countertop is fairly common except for sit-down vanities. Wheelchairs can generally access a 29" countertop height. This is the height of a typical desk.

On the other hand, people with osteoporosis can't stand erect and necessarily need a lower countertop height.

Some people may need to sit on a stool, bench, or chair at the sink in the kitchen or bath in order to access them.

Then, you have height differentials in a household where one person is taller and prefers one height for the counter and another shorter person likes something else. In the bathroom this can be accomplished with two vanities. In the kitchen, a single countertop height (whatever that might be) is generally chosen.

An adjustable countertop that I mentioned (motorized or manual) might be a solution for part of the kitchen.

Kitchen Desk

A sit-down desk that can be installed inline in a base cabinet run or separately along another wall in the kitchen — as a standalone or along with other base cabinets (and often with upper cabinets or shelving) is a concept that many people already use.

Once marketed as a "recipe desk," it now serves as the more commonly referenced "kitchen desk."

This is a great universal design concept that has multiple uses for a variety of ages and abilities.

However, the kitchen area may need to be enlarged or reconfigured to allow the use of the kitchen desk — depending on where you want to use it and how you want it located in the room.

The desk can be entirely open with just a countertop covering the space — inline with other cabinets so that the desk space is virtually invisible.

It also can look more like a typical desk with a single desk drawer beneath the countertop — or two or more adjacent drawers (depending on the width of the opening or knee space).

The drawer or side-by-side drawers in this position may interfere with wheelchair access, however, if that is a concern.

The design can also have one or two of the drawer base cabinet units on either or both sides of the knee space much like a traditional desk.

The countertop can be the same height as the other countertop space in the kitchen, but it is more versatile at a lower height in the 30" range — or even at the 29" typical desktop height.

Since this is a fairly common feature in many kitchens, the design does not suggest anything unusual, and it fits right in.

Still, it allows wheelchair access as well as the ability for anyone else in the household (including grandkids doing their homework or playing games) to use this space.

It can be designed or used as a computer or TV/movie station (with a TV, desktop computer, notebook, or tablet) or just remain an open countertop for crafts, writing, meal planning, eating, meal or baking preparation (where doing it from a seated position is necessary or desired).

It can serve as an area for cooking with a small appliance (coffee maker, crockpot, toaster oven, microwave, or induction burner) at a lower counter height — or several other uses where a desktop is beneficial because of its height, openness, and accessibility.

It can accommodate wheelchair access and be used without any adaptation.

Depending on the size of the desk you want to create, and whether you want it to be a freestanding unit or inline with other base cabinets and the main countertop, you can purchase the cabinets and countertops from the home center store and install them yourself.

Otherwise, the services of a remodeler, carpenter, handyman, kitchen and bath designer, or interior designer will be required.

Sit-Down Vanity

This is similar in design and concept to the kitchen desk and has been used in the master bathrooms of many homes for years.

It has never gone out of style, but its popularity seems to rise and fall in new construction of production homes. You may already have one of these in your home — even if you don't use it that much or at all.

Like the kitchen desk, the sit-down vanity can be installed inline in a vanity base cabinet run or separately along another wall in the bath — as a standalone.

Also like the kitchen desk, the sit-down vanity can be entirely open with just a countertop covering the space, or it can have one or more desk drawers immediately under the countertop (depending on the width of the opening — knee space).

It can even be built to look like a desk with vertical drawer units installed along one or both sides of the knee space. Again, the drawer may interfere with wheelchair access, however, if that is a concern.

As a universal design feature, the sit-down vanity, which is typically installed in the master bathroom (or occasionally in a dressing area near the bath), can also be used in the guest or secondary bathrooms for grandchildren, visiting adult children, or other houseguests to use for their grooming needs.

A typical desktop height is 29" and many bathroom vanities are built to this height. They range all the way up to 36". Some people like the sit-down portion of the vanity to be at the same height as the rest of the bathroom base cabinets, while others prefer it to be slightly to definitely lower.

While the height of the sit-down vanity can vary, the concept of the sit-down portion itself is a nice universal design feature that is widely used.

Again, depending on the size and complexity of the project, you may desire to purchase the cabinets and countertops from the home center store and install them — if you don't already have one in place.

Otherwise, the services of a remodeler, carpenter, handyman, kitchen and bath designer, or interior designer will be required.

Up-Front Controls

Certain appliances already are created with their operating controls and digital displays mounted on their front panels — the front-loading washing machine, automatic dishwasher, microwave oven, and induction cooktop are examples of this.

Many appliances can be switched out for ones more accessible when it comes time to replace them, and you can do this or use a remodeler or handyman to do this.

This is one area where you can really make life easier and more convenient for yourself and the others in your home.

There is more than just the controls and displays that need to be at or on the front of the appliances. The latches and doors do as well.

In addition to front-loading washing machines, dishwashers, cooktops, microwaves, and ovens that already are commonly available with up-front controls, many other appliances need to be selected with this in mind. This includes clothes dryers, laundry sinks, ranges, garbage disposals, range hoods, and exhaust fans.

Some of the changes will require moving or adding switches, gas lines, or plumbing, and an electrician or plumber may need to get involved also.

Easy-Access Appliances

Kitchen and other major appliances are used in your home every day so we need to look at making them more accessible and useable by everyone in your home.

The appliances that come to mind that have great solutions already available are front-loading washing machines, refrigerators, microwave ovens, cooktops, ranges, and dishwashers.

Others need to be selected or installed with universal design and accessibility in mind.

The front-loading automatic clothes washing machine has the controls and the door located on the front so that anyone can use it. It can even be raised with a pedestal base if it needs to be a little higher for members of the household.

A top loading washing machine does not provide these advantages. The door is on top and must be pulled up to open it. The controls are at the back and require reaching to access them. Then the clothes must be lifted to be placed into the machine, while the wet clothes must be lifted from the machine to dry them. These require good hand and arm strength and range-of-motion. Shorter people are going to have some difficulty with access. People in a wheelchair will have no access.

Refrigerators come in two styles that offer great accessibility — the side-by-side and the french-door models. In the french-door style with two doors (often equally sized) that close to the middle and open outward in either direction, the top shelves are going to be harder for someone short, seated, or with limited range-of-motion to reach.

However, there are models available with either two separate bottom drawers or with a drawer within a drawer.

Often one of these drawers has the option of serving as a refrigerator compartment in addition to being set as a freezer. Set to the refrigerator mode, access would be available for people unable to reach higher shelves in the refrigerator.

Water and ice in the door are a great feature that saves opening the door. Some models have a small access door on the right side that can be opened easily also.

Some cooktops have the controls on the surface along the front edge or in the lower corner of them. Induction cooktops have the touch controls along the front edge but on the surface of the cooktop.

Ranges (gas and electric) have their controls on the front facing out so they are easily accessible, and some knobs are actually red.

Dishwashers are accessible to all — either the traditional model with the door opening down and the pull-out baskets or the newer style with two drawers that open independently. They work well for someone in a wheelchair or seated.

As for appliances that need to be selected or installed with accessibility in mind, the oven when it is part of a range is fine (but the broiler part is often too low). When the oven is mounted in the wall apart from the stove or range, it needs to be at a useable height.

Finding and selecting an oven with a side-opening door (hinged along the side rather than the bottom) provides more safety, convenience and accessibility than one that opens down. Just be aware of extra clearance that may be required for the door to open safely.

For double ovens (or separate microwave and wall oven mounted vertically over each other), the top unit tends to be quite high for many people. Care should be taken to lower it and to make sure the controls and display are at eye-level or below.

Many newer clothes dryers have the controls mounted on the front, but some still have them at the back.

Ideally, locate the washer and dryer so that the doors close toward each other (opposing). This way, you can take clothes from the washer and put them right into the dryer without moving much or at all. Keep in mind the access and maneuvering room that might be required to safely use these appliances.

Microwaves are often mounted in line with the cabinets over the range. They typically have a range hood/exhaust fan function built into them also.

Because of where they are installed, it is difficult for many people to reach and use them or see the controls well due the height of them — especially when they have to reach over a stove or cooktop that could be in use.

People who are short, or those with range-of-motion or arm strength issues, face the additional challenge of removing hot food from the microwave and trying to set it down safely.

Some microwaves are installed with them directly resting on the countertop. While this brings them to a very useable and accessible level, countertop space is often forfeited.

As for range hoods, look for ones with a remote control that can operate the exhaust fan and the task lights that often are a part of them no matter how high they are installed — or have a switch for each (fan and lights) installed on the front edge of the countertop.

Many homeowners and renters can replace appliances on their own or with the help of an installer from the store where the appliances are purchased. Some professional assistance might be needed from a plumber, handyman, remodeler, or interior designer.

Easy-Access Faucets

In addition to having user-friendly and accessible appliances in your kitchen, bathrooms, and laundry room — including up-front controls — another universal design feature that goes along with this strategy is having the water faucets near the front of the sink or countertop.

However, this isn't always practical or desirable.

They can't look awkward and out-of-place suggesting that they are only there because someone has difficulty reaching them in their traditional location at the back of the sink.

Also, there may not be sufficient room to install the faucet due to the space required for the water supply lines — particularly in kitchens. This may interfere with adjacent cabinets and simply be impractical.

For kitchen or bathroom sinks (or pedestal or wall-hung sinks) that come with the holes already punched or formed into them in the traditional position at the back of the sink, this strategy of moving them forward and along the left or right side of the sink toward the front just would not work.

For bathroom vessel sinks and kitchen integrated bowl sinks where there is sufficient room to the side of the bowls to run water supply lines without encroaching on adjacent cabinets, however, a forward located single-lever faucet can be a good universal design feature.

These water supply lines will need to be wrapped under the sink to keep people from bumping into them since they are in a location different than where people normally expect them to be.

For laundry sinks and sinks on islands, this strategy of locating the faucets along the side and toward the front increases access to the faucets since these sinks tend to be deeper (as is the case with the laundry sink) or located farther back from the front of the countertop (as is often true with island sinks).

Wall Blocking

Wall blocking by itself — adding dimensional lumber (2" x 6", 2" x 8", 2" x 10", or 2" x 12" boards even though the 2" inch dimension is really only 1½" and the other dimensions are somewhat smaller also) horizontally and flush between the vertical wall studs to provide material into which to anchor a future installation of grab bars or other devices — is not a universal design strategy.

However, it is an adaptable strategy that will facilitate the later installation of towel bars, grab bars, or other items that need to be anchored securely to the wall without being concerned about locating a stud or working with products that may not fit exactly where the studs are located.

It also eliminates the need to rely on wall fasteners.

Using wider boards (say a 10" or 12" board versus a 6" one) provides more flexibility in choosing an appropriate mounting height.

Using plywood sheathing (⅝" or ¾") across the studs will work, but it doesn't provide the thickness of 2" lumber (again, normally 1½" although labeled as 2" thick) and reduces the functional size of the room by its thickness since the drywall needs to go on top of it rather than applied directly to the wall studs as is the case with dimensional lumber blocking.

If you are doing your own remodeling, you can handle this. Otherwise, a handyman, carpenter, or remodeler can do this work.

Windows

Every home has windows, but there's a lot more to consider than just having them. This is an area of your home that often goes unnoticed or overlooked in a remodeling project, but it is extremely important for many reasons — safety, comfort, security, and convenience, for instance.

Replacing windows is a task for the professional carpenter, contractor, window installer, or remodeler.

People generally select their home in part by the size and location of windows. They look for how well the windows add natural light to a space and how that varies throughout the day, the ability of the windows to provide ventilation and fresh air when they are opened, the view the windows offer from various rooms, how the windows might suggest furniture placement in a room (in a bedroom, family room, living room, dining room, or kitchen), and the way the size and shape of the windows fit into the exterior design.

Windows generally come with the home and are not specifically selected for how accessible they are or how easy they are to open. This often isn't discovered until after living in the home with your own furniture in place where you normally use it.

Some windows are not as accessible or easy to open as might have been thought once cabinetry or furniture is in front of them — partially blocking them or creating a barrier to reaching them.

Also, how far someone might need to reach, how much hand and arm strength they may need, or the range-of-motion required to push the window sash open or operate the crank are additional considerations that may not immediately come to mind.

Depending on what your local building codes require as a minimum height of a window from the floor, windows that provide easy viewing through them from a seated position are at a good height for everyone.

At such a height, anyone can access them as well for egress in an emergency and for emergency personnel to gain entry. This attribute of windows is often overlooked.

Thus, a relatively low window — in terms of distance of the sill from the floor — is a universal design feature because anyone can see through the glass and observe what is happening outside or enjoy the view.

The lower the windows are in relation to the floor, the easier they are going to be to open, but it's not just a matter of reaching the crank or the sash.

For safety, security, and comfort, the window sash needs to be latched securely.

For casement windows, the latch that secures the windows is usually located along the side of the window. Look for and select windows with the latch near the bottom or actually along the bottom rather than halfway up the side of the sash.

You can also find casement windows where the handle that secures them just turns 90° to unlatch them. There is nothing to turn or crank in or out. Once unlatched, the windows simply push out or pull it to open them.

Contrast this with single-hung and double-hung windows where the latching/locking mechanism is on top of the lower window sash or frame.

Sometimes security pins can be installed lower on the sash — in place of the lock at the top of the sash — by drilling through the sash and into the frame in one or more places to keep the window from opening or to keep it opened securely at a pre-determined amount.

Depending on the size of the windows, how high they are installed from the floor, how heavy they are, and how difficult they are to open and close, a short person, your grandchild, someone in a wheelchair, someone with range-of-motion issues in their upper body, or someone without a lot of hand and arm strength or abdominal muscle strength may be unable to release or operate the windows.

Pay attention to the actual operation of opening the window once it is unlatched — the ease or difficulty in turning the crank to open a casement window or raising the lower sash of a single- or double-hung window.

You may decide to replace your single- or double-hung windows if you have them and use only casement windows — a solid window panel framed by wood, wood with vinyl cladding, or aluminum that opens on a pivot horizontally or vertically, depending on the style selected.

This will eliminate reaching and range-of-motion concerns for opening and closing the windows.

As I mentioned, you might want to select windows that unlatch and push outward or pull inward (horizontal and vertical pivots are available) to open them rather than needing to be cranked into an open position.

Whatever you select, make sure they are lightweight yet durable and that you and others in your home can operate them easily and safely.

Adding impact resistance glass will be beneficial and universal also for safety, security, and convenience – and peace of mind against possible intruders, mischief, vandalism, or wind storms.

Motorized Window Coverings

Window coverings are a personal design choice. People can use curtains, drapes, shades, shutters, or blinds – or a combination of treatments. These can vary throughout the home as well. Some people use nothing.

Sometimes the window treatments are installed and never touched again. Some are adjusted to keep out the bright daylight or to let in more light on cloudy days. Privacy and security are reasons for closing blinds and drapes as well.

Someone's height, range-of-motion, and hand and arm strength might factor into how well they can operate curtain and blinds controls.

So, here is a state-of-the-art feature a little like the body dryer that we looked at on page 118. While not everyone is going want to include this feature in their home or determine that they have a need for it, it is a universal design treatment that is applicable to any design.

It fits in and is not noticeable as anything special or unusual. This is a remote controlled window treatment.

The blinds or shades can be raised or lowered without physically touching them or being next to them. Someone from across the room (standing, seated, or in wheelchair), could operate them.

In addition to just adjusting the height of the blinds or shades, the blinds can be adjusted to the fully opened position (90° or horizontal), the partially opened position, or the closed position (flat). They will remain that way until they are changed.

A similar feature is a remote controlled window motor

that can open and close casement windows or skylights. This accommodates people of all sizes and abilities.

You will likely need a remodeler or electrician to install these motors for you to make sure they are working properly.

Elevators

Elevators are in a class by themselves.

They aren't what we typically think of as a universal design feature, concept, or strategy, and they don't apply to ranch-style or single-level homes unless there is a basement or a major increase in grade from the street or driveway to the front door of your home.

Nevertheless, in multi-level homes they can be used by people that don't climb stairs well or by anyone else. In that sense, they are universal.

With two-story homes (or more), there may be a great opportunity for adaptable design by creating an elevator shaft for future use.

Maybe you already have a bedroom or hallway closet on each floor situated one on top of the other.

Possibly you already have an elevator also — or you've already made plans to install one.

If not, look for the opportunity to design and create a space for one in the event you desire it later.

The closet space needs to be large enough for an elevator car so be sure to plan for this.

Then, whenever an elevator is desired, simply remove the ceiling of the first floor closet (which is the floor of the second floor closet) to create a cavity or shaft to house the elevator. Make sure that the landing and approach room is sufficient to operate the elevator.

The ceiling/floor that is being removed would be designed in such a way that it could be taken out for this purpose.

The closet doors can remain, but they should not interfere with getting on or off the elevator.

Even when it's not possible to align the two closets to create an elevator shaft, an elevator still might be a safety, comfort, convenient, and accessible design choice to include in your home.

There also are elevators that can be installed outside the structure and attached and finished in such a way as to give the appearance that the home was designed and built with that feature included. From the exterior, it is about the same size and appearance as an enclosed and finished stairwell.

There are free-standing tubular elevators that can be used in spaces where a larger elevator wouldn't work or when a solution is desired without a lot of construction.

These can go as high as three floors, and they can be used by either going through a floor to the next level or by going alongside the floor in the case of a loft.

There are different primary energy sources available for elevators, but look for back-up batteries or how the unit can be powered by a back-up generator when there is a power outage.

Whatever solution you select in terms of an elevator, this is strictly a professional installation. A DME (durable medical equipment) supplier or consultant would be a good resource.

Spiral Stairways

If you have a home that was built with a spiral staircase or stairway — possibly used to access your master bedroom, a loft, a library, or a den while keeping the footprint of the staircase to a minimum, you may find that the stairway is now very difficult to use.

It may have been practical at one time, but now you find using it is not something you like doing.

They are narrow and wind from the bottom to the top.

Anyone with balance issues, range-of-motion limitations in the hips or legs, a bad back, sore feet, joint issues, or poor stamina would not be able to use the spiral stairway effectively.

A solution is to remove the spiral stairway and replace it with a pneumatic tubular elevator that fits in roughly the same space and sits right on the main floor. You can stand or sit in the elevator as it moves between floors.

It can go through the ceiling where the spiral staircase is. For a loft or bridge area, the tubular elevator can go along side it without needing to go through the floor.

Regular Stairways

If you have a two-story home or more, or one with a basement, you have stairs. You might also have an elevator, but you have stairs.

As long as we aren't talking about a winding grand central staircase that has no walls along its sides, there are ways to adapt stairways to make them accessible to anyone.

There are chair lifts (for people who can sit in a chair while it moves them up and down stairs), platform lifts (for people who can remain sitting in their wheelchair or standing with their walker), and elevators (that can move people between floors).

Whenever some other treatment is used in a stairway, such as a lift of some type, or an auxiliary elevator separate from the stairs is created, the stairs actually remain in place. No one is suggesting removal of the stairs.

Lifts and elevators are not universal designs because they are a visible improvement to the home for a specific use. Nevertheless, they can be used and accessed by many people — those in your home as well as guests, and others with minor discomforts that enjoy the assistance to those with more severe limitations that actually require it.

Make sure from a safety and comfort standpoint that all stairs are fully enclosed (the treads and the risers). Many basements steps are open along the back — allowing the possibility that someone might twist their ankle or catch their foot (and then fall) by sticking their foot into the open space.

Also, you want sure, safety footing on the stair treads themselves to prevent someone from slipping on them.

Dumbwaiters/Clothes Chute

This is a little like an elevator for items and articles. As long as it is installed so that it is at an accessible height, it is a great universal design feature.

Of course, like the elevator, the dumbwaiter only works in multiple floor homes or single story homes with a basement.

Rather than carrying items up and down stairs — for those who might have limited strength or holding power, those with balance or coordination issues, those with poor stamina, or those using assistance — this is a great solution. Simply put the items in the dumbwaiter car and send them up or down to the next level. They can even remain on the carry until someone goes up or down to retrieve them later.

They don't have a particularly large footprint, but some construction is going to be involved in installing this. A remodeler, contractor, occupational therapist, kitchen and bath designer, DME provider, and electrician are resources for you.

A similar idea to the dumbwaiter — but one without moving parts — is the clothes chute. This feature has been around for years — again for multiple story homes or basement homes.

The principle of this feature is that clothes, after they have been worn or used (such as towels and linens) are dropped into the clothes chute for a direct ride to the laundry room (on the first floor or basement) — depending on where the washing machine is located. Gravity is the engine for this.

Chair Lifts

Like the elevator, having a chair lift applies to two-or-more-story homes or ones with a basement. There have to be stairs for this to work, and it's an alternative for moving people between floors.

These don't replace the stairs except for the people who need the lift to get up or down to the next level. The physical stairs still remain.

Chair lifts themselves are not a universal design feature. Neither are platform lifts for people who need to be transported between levels (or even from the outside to the entrance of your home) while remaining in their wheelchairs.

Nevertheless, installing a chair lift may be desirable for someone who has moderate mobility (hip, knee, ankle, or feet issues), stamina, breathing, or balance issues.

The main consideration in putting in a chair lift — aside from the fact that there needs to be a stairway — is that someone must be able to access the chair, sit down on it (even if transferring from a wheelchair or walker), remain sitting on it as it climbs or descends stairs, and get off it safely.

An electric outlet located at the base of the stairs and the landing — even if not required by the building code

— will mean that a chair lift could be installed at a future date if necessary or desired.

In the meantime, one can never have too many outlets. An outlet located here would facilitate plugging in decorative holiday lights and using the vacuum or other electrical appliances in this area of the home.

Just make sure with any type of remodeling that is done on or around the base of the stairs that sufficient floor space is maintained to accommodate the chair lift track. It rests on the floor and extends well past the base of the stairs — creating a potential tripping hazard if there is a walkway or hallway here.

If you are handy with home repairs (and can handle the weight of this product), you could likely install this yourself, but a professional can easily do it and make sure that it is operating correctly.

First-Floor Master Suite

Obviously, this applies to multi-story homes and townhomes. This is not an issue in ranch-style homes.

As people age, climbing stairs can become more of an issue for a number of different reasons, such as range-of-motion in their hips, knees, or ankles, foot issues, deteriorating joints, balance, stamina, coordination, and cardio-vascular function.

If your home is a multi-level one and does not have a bedroom of some type on the main floor, you will want to create a first floor master suite.

The market is very receptive to this idea so this will aid in resale when it comes time for that.

Even if you are able to climb stairs without difficulty now, or you plan on installing a lift or elevator (or you already have done so), there are many times when you might benefit from a first floor master bedroom — even if this is not the main place you sleep.

You might have family or close friends who visit overnight who need an accessible bedroom without climbing stairs or using a lift or elevator. Also, occasional illnesses, surgeries, or injuries may affect members of your household, and going up the stairs to their bedroom may not be feasible or easy.

This is going to require professional help to accomplish — especially to make sure a bathroom is connected to the bedroom. The space layout for the remainder of the main floor may have to change as well to accommodate the first-floor master suite.

Depending on the available space on the main floor and the ability to convert a den or study into a bedroom, this is likely a major undertaking. However, this is a safety, comfort, convenience, and accessible strategy.

The Upstairs Retreat

This is an intentional, strategic way of using the second or third floor of your home — for people who have multiple story homes. Whether you normally climb stairs to get to the second or third level of your home, or you rely on a lift or elevator, this strategy still applies.

Essentially this treats the second or third floor of your home as a destination — ideally when sleeping is done on the main floor.

It still works when the bedroom is on the upper floor, but the real reason for this strategy is to accommodate using the upper floor or floors for a specific lifestyle function while doing most of your living on the main floor. This reduces trips up and down stairs for people who have difficulty using the stairs but don't need to go upstairs to sleep.

You determine how much you want to use the upper floor or floors of your home — both in terms of days and hours. Say it's Monday, Wednesday, and Friday from 10:00 am-3:00 pm. Then you plan to go upstairs for those hours — and only those hours. That's how it becomes a destination.

Use it as a studio to write, paint, do crafts or puzzles, read, or anything you like. Just have an outing.

This upstairs space would be configured with a small kitchen and a bath. Just carve out enough space for the destination, and the rest can remain storage or bedrooms for visiting family or friends to use.

Heat or cool only the space you are using.

Two Master Suites

Years ago, many homes were built with just one bathroom for the entire home so these layouts did not have a master suite or ensuite where there is a private bathroom just for use by the master bedroom.

If your home does not have a master suite that includes a bathroom that you don't have to share with the rest of the home, that would be a great place to start in your remodeling.

Most of the bathroom features and treatments I have been presenting to you in this book are for the master bath.

So the first objective is to have a master suite with a bedroom and bathroom for yourself. Then we can consider adding a second one.

The second master suite has several advantages. When adult children visit (or move back in), they can use it. If a sibling, parent, or other relative visits or moves in with you, it will accommodate them — the same with other visiting houseguests. A visiting or live-in caregiver could use it also.

When minor illnesses, insomnia, post-surgery recovery, or other issues affect you or someone else in your family, it may be desirable to have separate quarters where you or they can retreat to and have privacy.

This may not be a high priority item on your list of remodeling projects, but it is universal and will add value to your home. Obviously this is a major construction project that will require the services of several professionals to accomplish,

Garage Access

In homes with an attached garage, there is a step-up from the garage floor to the main floor of your home. It might be a relatively small 4"-6" step up, or it could be as many as two or three constructed concrete or wooden steps.

Minimizing the impact of this grade differential for people with range-of-motion, balance, mobility, or other issues will make going from the garage to the home more comfortable and safe.

The difference in height between the garage floor and the floor of your home may be such that the only way to bridge the difference is with a ramp. Then there will need to be plenty of approach room to access the ramp plus a landing area with approach room to open the door to your home from the garage.

If the difference between the two levels is small, a small slope can be framed and poured with concrete to allow access between the two floors without a specific step up or down. Just make sure the run (length of the slope or small ramp) is long enough to be provide safe footing and eliminate the possible loss of balance in using it. Make sure that this bridge is not slippery.

Back-Up Power

Aside from occasional power outages from various causes, storms can disrupt electricity for brief periods of time — from a few seconds to several hours or days.

While comfort, convenience, accessibility, and safety are important considerations during a power outage due to such items as alarm systems, lighting (interior and exterior), heating and air conditioning, computers, TVs, appliances, and refrigeration, some medically necessary equipment may depend on electricity as well.

While fuel oil, propane, or natural gas may normally power some items in the home such as hot water and heating, an electrical outage will shut off lights, TVs, computers, and refrigerators — at a minimum.

Back-up generators are quite useful and universal for supplying electrical power needs when the normal power service is interrupted — they just are not practical for taking over the energy load of running your entire home (for more than a few hours) because of the size of the generator that would be required and the amount of energy required to run it and keep it going.

Generators can power many essential and necessary systems, appliances, and items in your home — just not all of the energy needs in your home without a large capacity generator and a large, limitless, dependable power source.

Natural gas could be considered a large, limitless power source, but it can be somewhat expensive to run your entire house with it by powering your generator for several days.

If chair lifts, platform lifts, or elevators are present in your home — or you plan on installing them — they likely have back-up power designed into them. If not, the back-up generator installed for your other energy needs would operate them.

Even a UPS (uninterruptible power supply) battery like you use for your computer can provide temporary backup for a few uses of a power bed or chair lift.

A back-up generator is something an electrician needs to

install along with a remodeler or handyman so that it engages automatically when it is supposed to and powers those systems or devices that are important.

Installing the generator wrong could be an inefficient energy drain by running too many devices (or the wrong circuits) and very dangerous by backflowing power onto the electrical grid.

Indoor Air Quality

Many people suffer from allergies, and there is more attention being paid to indoor air quality — particularly as the building envelop is being designed and created to be tighter.

Using low- or no-VOC paints, glues, adhesives, and building materials — or ones that don't off-gas — are being requested by an increasing segment of the population.

Eliminating carpeting, as I mentioned, is a positive step in improving indoor air quality because of the way it's made and the way it traps and hold dust and allergens.

I already mentioned the automatic dustpan port also.

Built-ins are attractive, but they are dust-catchers. Niches, bookcases, open beams, large window sills and ledges, decorative columns with fluted surfaces, and many other building accessories and finishes add aesthetically to a home's interior but also present indoor air quality issues in terms of attracting dust or allowing dust to settle and remain on them.

They aren't always the easiest to vacuum or wipe off either.

I'm not talking about your personal furniture — just design or architectural elements that may have been added to your home.

A cleaner, easier-to-maintain look will promote better indoor air quality (while possibly sacrificing some aesthetic treatments).

Determine if there are design elements in your home that seem to be unusual dust catchers or those that might be hard to reach and clean. Also, keep this in mind when designing future improvements.

6

Universal Design On The Outside

Why Look At The Exterior?

In addition to all of the improvements, changes, modifications, strategies, and new installations you can make or have done on the inside of your home to create universal accessibility, safety, convenience, security, and comfort, there are many ways to improve the exterior of your home as well.

This applies whether you rent or own your home and whether it's a single family detached structure or a semi-attached/detached home such as a duplex, villa, or townhome.

Before you ever get inside your home or apartment, you need to have safe access and approach on the outside.

The principles of universal design and accessibility don't just magically begin once you or your visitors or guests open the front door and enter your living space.

They begin at the curb and continue along your entry sidewalks and driveway to the front door.

Here are a few ideas and things to keep an eye on to get you started creating an accessible and safe living environment from the outside-in.

Zero-Step/Barrier-Free Entrances

In some parts of the country, building codes may not allow a true zero-step entrance into your home that is at grade level (with no noticeable change from the entrance walk to the main floor of your home).

However, there may other ways to accomplish this through a gentle sloping or ramping that bridges the few inches that the threshold needs to be above grade for flooding concerns or other issues.

Make sure you or your contractor follow the local building codes in terms of what is required or allowed in terms of making a zero-step threshold or entry — even if you don't get a building permit for the work.

The concept of a zero-step or barrier free entry is to allow anyone easy, unrestricted access to your home, whether it's you, other household members, your guests or your visitors (invited or not), or your grandchildren — from young to old and walking unaided, using a walker or wheelchair, being pushed in a baby carriage or stroller, using a wheeled toy, or just having range-of-motion limitations, joint issues, or foot problems that makes stepping up and down difficult.

Nevertheless, everyone will need to step on or over the wooden or metal threshold against which the entry door closes. The concept of barrier free is to reduce and eliminate other steps and barriers along the entry walk — from the driveway or street to the entrance of your home.

Even when small changes in grade (steps) can't be totally eliminated because of the building code or physical elements of your yard, they can adapted to minimize their impact.

In some cases, an attractive, well-constructed, and well-landscaped ramp may be used as universal access to your home — or in addition to steps or another type of approach that might be present. A longer ramp will keep the angle of rise (slope) to a minimum and make it more comfortable for anyone to use it.

Well-done ramps can provide an alternative entry without necessarily calling attention to their presence — whether they are required for accessibility or not.

Some jurisdictions consider ramps to be permanent structures that must have a building permit and be inspected. However, most places do not have this requirement so you can design them as you like.

Entry Steps/Stoop/Porch

Each home is different as far as how someone approaches the front door and accesses it. Homes are often somewhat similar in a given neighborhood because of when or by whom they were built, however.

The concern with the concrete pad or stoop outside the front door or the wooden or poured concrete porch is that it provides safe footing and enough access room and maneuverability for people to approach the front door and open it or allow it to be opened for them to pass through it.

If you have a small stoop that is 3' x 3' or similar, this generally is not large enough for someone to open the storm door outward and get out of the way of it. It's even more of a challenge for someone using a wheelchair, cane, or walker — and someone may have balance issues also.

Pay particular attention to how the stoop or porch is protected. Often, there are no railings to keep someone from failing off the sides of the surface. This is a significant safety risk.

It's important from a safety, comfort, and convenience standpoint to have a porch, front patio, landing area, approach zone, stoop, or pad at the front door that is large enough to allow more than one person to gather while waiting for you or someone else in your home to open the door for them and also allow them to maneuver out of the way of the door opening out (for entrance doors that might open out and for screen or storm doors).

To exit and leave your home — whether it's you, someone else in your household, or a visitor or guest — the same is true.

People walk out the door and then stop to make sure they have everything with them that they are supposed to before going on their way.

Make sure that the surface of your patio, stoop, or porch provides sufficient traction to keep you, your family, and your guests or visitors from slipping during inclement weather.

Entry steps, when they are present — whether it's just a minor step up from the sidewalk onto the stoop or patio (or step down going the other way) or several steps, wooden or concrete — create their own safety, comfort, convenience, visitability, and accessibility issues. They are not universal because there are many people who cannot use them safely — or at all.

You will need to look at safe alternatives for your entrance steps if you currently have them. This should be a relatively high priority for your personal safety and those of people who visit you.

Seek the assistance of professionals to help you design and create a safer, more accessible entryway.

Sidewalks

Many homes are built without much attention to the sidewalks leading from the street to the front door or from the driveway to the front door.

Sometimes a basic walkway is formed and poured — or one is created with brick pavers or stepping stones (concrete pavers) — without much attention to function.

Some homes don't even have a formal sidewalk — they just have a path, with or without stepping stones.

The dirt path can become muddy, and those with stepping stones can become overgrown with grass and difficult to use because of the spacing between them or the fact that they are broken or pitched in various directions.

Many dirt paths and hard surface sidewalks retain water during a rain or lawn sprinkling.

Some walkways have intermediate steps and may or may not have railings for assistance.

A much more strategic, accessible, and visitable approach to designing a sidewalk is to make it wide enough for easy use by grandchildren playing, for people using a walker or wheelchair, for moving furniture or equipment in and out of the home, or for two or more people to walk side-by-side (either going along together or coming and going in opposite directions) on the walkway.

Also take into account creating a non-slip surface (under most conditions), the rise and slope of the walkway (eliminating steps whenever possible), installing it slightly above grade for better drainage (if the building code allows it), and making it easy to use in terms of twists and turns. There might even need to be one or more flat intermediate landings.

Also, the type of landscaping and other obstacles along the walkway are important safety considerations to keep in mind with the possibility of someone veering from the hard surface and injuring themself.

Designing, forming, pouring, and finishing your walkway is something for the professionals to do — landscape architect, flatwork contractor, cement finisher, remodeler, occupational therapist, architect, or handyman.

Remember to include radiant heating in your sidewalk remodeling plans unless you are in a warm climate.

Ramps

Ramps are not purely a universal design element because they do have a relatively large footprint and aren't unobtrusive — they are quite visible.

This does not mean that they can't be used by everyone, however. Nearly anyone of any age or ability can walk or use assistance to get themselves up and down a ramp.

In most local jurisdictions, ramps are not governed by building or zoning codes. Therefore, you can build or use what you like.

If you need to install a ramp specifically for yourself or others in your home, you can participate in the size, length, shape, and location of it — even if you create a new entranceway into your home just for the ramp.

Consider the length of time the ramp likely will need to be used (use your best guess, or design it for several years if you aren't sure). This will help you select the appropriate materials to use and might also factor into where you decide to locate it. The next owner of your home may appreciate having it also — especially if it's designed well and attractively landscaped.

This might be the primary entrance into your home or a secondary one — depending on where you place it and how you design it. It could replace an existing walkway or be used in addition to it.

It can blend into your overall landscaping by placing a hedge, bushes, a planter, or a knee wall (brick, stone, stucco, or siding to match your home) along the ramp on the side visible from the street to create a more unobtrusive look that just fits in. This will also add a little more privacy for those using the ramp.

Remember to follow the appropriate guidelines for the slope of the ramp (even though this is not a requirement in most cases) and to install curbing, sides of some type, a lower secondary railing, and some type of transition (appropriate for the surface, such as a rubber insert, sanded treads, sandblasting, or etching) at each end of the ramp to aid in traction.

Depending on your skill level and ability, you might be able to create this, but it is likely that you will require professional assistance to complete it.

Entry Shelves/Tables/Furniture

A universal design strategy that definitely appeals to all ages and abilities and addresses safety, comfort, convenience, and accessibility issues is an outdoor entry shelf or piece of furniture such as a table.

This is installed or placed next to the entrance (the latch side or door handle side of the front door — unless you use the side door or back door as much or more than the front door and it can apply to these doors also).

This is another reason for having a large enough stoop, patio, or porch at your entrance.

The shelf, table, stand, or other piece of furniture should be somewhat lower in height than the door handle so as not to interfere with its function and safe operation.

You can use most any dimension that you like, but it should be large enough and deep enough to be functional without be so big that it is obtrusive or a barrier to entering safely.

Depending on its size and shape, it might provide storage space inside or underneath it or allow for a small sculpture or plant on top.

It can be wood or metal and can be painted, stained, or decorated as you like to be compatible with the general design, theme, and colors of your home or entry porch. It can even make a statement.

It's quite common to get out of the car and walk up to the front door with your hands full of various things.

This may not be an all-the-time occurrence, but often you might be carrying the mail, an umbrella, a jacket that you aren't wearing, groceries, packages, shopping bags, books, tools, dry cleaning, a briefcase, purse, small grandchildren, a cup of coffee or a soft drink, fast food (that you are still eating or in the bag to eat once inside), or a cell phone.

Maybe you are trying to assist someone else to get into your home or show attention to a pet that greets you.

Then, with your hands full of what you are carrying or attending to, you need to look for your keys, make or take a phone call, keep from dropping something you have been carrying that is beginning to slip, or have a hand free to open the door.

Even if you aren't driving but are simply bringing in the mail or things from the yard, the shelf can be helpful.

Having a shelf or object (such as a table or stand) to set things on makes perfect sense rather than juggling them, trying to balance them, or setting them on the ground.

Just make sure that whatever you decide to use — a shelf, cabinet, stand, table, or other object or piece of furniture —that it is painted or otherwise treated to withstand precipitation if it is in an area that might get wet (directly or from windblown rain or snow).

Covered Entry/Guttering

When you arrive at your front door — or you have guests or visitors that come to your front door — it should be dry, even if it is snowing or raining right up until you or your guests arrive at the door.

This is a safety, comfort, and convenience solution that definitely appeals to all ages and abilities.

You and your guests or visitors need to be sheltered from rain or snow when it is present so you can pause in a dry area immediately before entering your home without being subjected to the precipitation.

This gives you and your visitors time to compose yourself as you shake off the rain or snow, take off your raincoat, clean off your boots or shoes, or shake off and fold up your umbrella — whether you first have to unlock the door or just open it and enter.

Most entrances have an overhang of sorts, but at a minimum guttering should be installed to keep the precipitation from running off the roof and onto you or your guests — generally at a fairly heavy flow — when you or they approach the door.

It also — if it is installed correctly — will collect and drain the water away from the sidewalk or driveway that you and your guests will use to approach the front door — keeping everyone's feet dryer and providing safer, surer footing on the walkway and more accessibility without having to navigate around puddles or slippery spots on the walkway.

A covered entry or porch (that also has guttering along the edge of it for the reasons just mentioned) provides even more protection and shelter.

Then with the entry shelf, stand, table, or other piece of furniture I mentioned, you can set down anything you are holding while you open the door.

Again, you can see and appreciate the importance of a sufficiently large area outside the entrance door.

You might be able to install the guttering that you get from the home center store.

However, a covered entry is likely a job for a handyman, carpenter, or remodeler — possibly an architect or roofer if it is particularly large or will be tied into the existing roofline.

Door Closers

The concept of an automatic door closer sounds attractive for people with poor arm strength or range-of-motion that might have difficulty in holding onto a door as they opened it to walk through or in reaching for it to close it — or for those using a wheelchair or walker.

However, there are a couple of considerations. An automatic door opener is not totally a universal design element — almost.

Small grandchildren could activate the door just to see it open, and someone close to the door but unaware that it was about to open might be struck by it.

If someone is relatively slow on their feet or uses a wheelchair or other mobility assistance such as a walker or cane, the time for the door to remain open would need to be adjusted and set for a longer sequence.

A manual switch to activate the door to return to its closed position is likely the best solution when the door closer serves as an effective solution otherwise.

This is likely something for an electrician, remodeler, or other professionals to install for you.

Radiant Heating

In areas where temperatures are cold enough for ice and snow to be present, a universal design feature and treatment that provides safety, comfort, convenience, and accessibility is radiant heating in the concrete sidewalks (front, back, and side), driveways, entrance stoops, and patios around the home so that the ice and snow are melted and the possibility of slipping or having unsure footing is greatly reduced or eliminated.

This also will keep wet patches of melted snow or ice or other precipitation (rain or sleet) from freezing when the temperature drops low enough.

This obviously is a major renovation project and will require the services of people such as a remodeler, flatwork contractor, HVAC contractor, cement mason, architect, and landscape architect to produce an attractive, effective result.

Unloading/Landing Area

This is something that isn't given much thought until there is a need for it.

This definitely applies to homes with single-car driveways, ones with normal two-car driveways, and those without a complete solid surface driveway.

For homes with very wide two-car driveways (more than just the width of the garage), the driveways likely can accommodate people unloading from a vehicle without stepping in the grass, dirt, or planting area along the sides of the driveway, and no other work may be desired or required.

For the rest of the driveways, this universal design treatment should be implemented.

Generally, being able to unload your car, van, or truck from the passenger side onto a hard surface would only be true if the vehicle was parked to the left side of the driveway with the right side being used for the loading and unloading area.

This is why this doesn't work at all for single-car driveways.

For increased safety, convenience, comfort, visitability, and accessibility, the driveway — regardless of its current width (but definitely for single-car and normal two-car driveways) — should be enlarged along the right side of the driveway (facing it from the street) with a hard, all-weather surface of concrete or pavers to allow plenty of firm footing for all passengers to disembark from their vehicle (wherever it is parked on the driveway) and to allow plenty of space for a walker or wheelchair to be unloaded, set up, and used.

This extra loading and unloading space is beneficial for everyone — especially on inclement days or when the vehicle needs to be loaded with luggage, supplies, pets, boxes, or other objects in addition to the occupants of the vehicle. Think of unloading groceries, home improvement supplies, or other items after an afternoon of shopping and running errands.

For vans with ramps that extend from the vehicle (to allow people in wheelchairs or those with other mobility issues to safely enter and exit the vehicle), there needs to be space for the ramp to deploy and for people to still be on a hard surface while entering or after leaving the van.

Everything that holds true for your household members would also apply to visitors and guests.

If anyone in your home needs the services of a van or private bus service to go to the doctor or be transported other places, there wouldn't be any concern about where the van or bus parked in the driveway because there would still be a hard-surface approach access.

When the approach area is not needed for passenger unloading or loading, the extra driveway space can be used for parking (cars, motorcycles, golf carts, or bicycles), as a place to wash your car, as a seating area with lawn chairs, or as a relatively clean play area for your grandchildren.

You've likely seen other people who have added an additional parking area onto their driveway for additional vehicles, but this is a universal design strategy that accommodates that but primarily exists for the safety, comfort, convenience, visitability, and accessibility of you and your guests.

If you like. you can add landscaping (flowers, mulch, and bushes) around the landing area to give the rain a place to drain and make it look more like an integral feature of your home and less like an afterthought.

This extra width can be just as practical when not needed for getting in and out of the vehicles which is why this is a universal design and visitable strategy.

Think of how your visitors are going to respond to this if they need the extra space to enter or leave their vehicle.

Be sure to include radiant heating in this also because sure footing is very important for this feature.

Lighting

I already mentioned and discussed photo cells, timers, and motion sensors earlier.

These all work outside as well as indoors provided they can withstand the elements or are used in a relatively dry or covered area (such as on a porch or covered entry, or under the eaves or overhang).

Another type of lighting (in a variety of sizes and styles) that can be used outdoors — anywhere you desire it for security, comfort, peace-of-mind, and general appearance — is a solar powered one.

It can be a yard or house light — utilitarian or decorative — that stays on all night or one that just comes on when it detects motion — depending on what type of light is selected and what the objective is.

The principal advantage to this type of light is that it can be located anywhere on the property because it does not need to be wired into or plugged into electricity.

It draws its energy from batteries that are recharged by the sun.

Of course, the solar collector that recharges the batteries needs to be in a place where it can receive sunlight. Over a prolonged cloudy, rainy, or snowy period (a few days or longer) the batteries will drain, but they will recharge once the sun comes back.

Also, locate it away from tree branches or other objects that might block the sunlight from reaching the solar collector.

Yard Sprinklers/Hoses

Yard sprinklers, hoses, and other tools that are used to care for the grass, garden, flowers, and landscaping are not universal design features, but there is a significant safety component here that needs to be addressed. That's why this section is included.

You might not do any outside work around your home such as mowing the grass, edging the walks, keeping a garden, or tending to bushes, shrubs, flowers, and trees.

You may not be able to do it, choose not to do it, or have a service that you use.

If you don't do any yardwork, then there isn't much cause for concern on your part.

However, if you do go out in your yard to maintain it, be careful of tripping hazards that arise from pop-up sprinkler heads on your irrigation system, sprinklers that you have deployed that are attached to hoses, hoses that might be lying in the grass (they might be partially concealed), branches that have fallen or that remain after being trimmed or pruned, and tools that may not have been picked up that might be partially hidden in the grass or landscaping.

Maintaining your yard needs to be done safely.

7

Summary Of Universal Design Treatments

Universal Design Makes A Positive Difference

I've been showing you various options, ideas, and solutions that are available for you to use in improving your home and adding to the overall lifestyle and enjoyment of all who live in your home.

This is the concept of universal design — making your living space (inside and out) as comfortable, convenient, safe, accessible, visitable, sustainable, and enjoyable as possible for you, others living in your home, and people who are just visiting.

Those visits could be just an hour or two for someone just dropping by or attending a function you are hosting, or they could be for a few days for overnight guests. In the case of visiting family, those stays could be longer than a week.

In addition to quality improvements that you get to see and experience in your home, universal design changes and treatments also add value to your home that you will realize when you go to sell it in the future.

Without an appraisal, there is no way to put a specific dollar amount on how much the value of your home will be improved with your universal design changes, but the fact that it literally will appeal to the broadest of audiences makes it generally desirable and worth more. It likely will sell quicker as a result.

An additional objective in universal design is to make the changes and treatments as invisible as possible so that they don't stand out or call attention to themselves except as something high tech, modern, contemporary, functional, or interesting to use.

People shouldn't notice that anything special has been done to accommodate or adapt your home for special needs unless that was your intent.

As far as making your home more livable, safe, and enjoyable, the design features that I have been suggesting to you will accomplish those objectives and fit right in as good design elements.

Universal Design Helps With
Special Needs And Aging

Universal design and special needs modifications are not the same thing, yet as I've shown in this book, good universal design concepts and strategies actually accommodates many special needs issues through its treatments and strategies.

This text has been looking at ways people can age comfortably in the home they have selected and get many years of enjoyment and satisfaction from their home.

As a design emphasis, universal design facilitates changes, improvements, solutions, and treatments that can provide a safer, more comfortable, more convenient, visitable, accessible, and secure home for you and those who share your home with you.

Regardless of any aging limitations or ailments, such as restricted range-of-motion, reduced stamina or endurance, changes in balance or coordination, sore or swollen joints, circulation, mobility, sensory, or other concerns, universal design enables us to live well in our homes and for our homes to remain safe for us.

For specific needs in addition to normal aging, you should find the universal design suggestions that I have given you to be helpful and a great place to start.

Universal design features — if they truly are designed for all ages (including seniors) and abilities (including restrictions and limitations brought on by age) — will let people with certain mobility, sensory, or cognitive issues function quite well in their surroundings the same as people without those concerns.

That's why these features are called universal design, and that's the big benefit of using them. They let essentially everyone live better in their homes.

They allow you and anyone else who lives in your home or visits you to experience comfortable, safe, accessible, intuitive, easy-to-use design choices in such facets of your home as lighting, controls, doors, cabinets, mirrors, faucets, shelving, appliances, entrances, walkways, passageways, flooring, and bathroom fixtures.

However, if you need a solution beyond what I have discussed in this text, an occupational therapist, physical therapist, DME (durable medical equipment) consultant, or other health care professional (HCP) should be consulted.

Universal Design Adds Value And Enjoyment

Whether the universal design changes in and around your home are made by you as the homeowner or tenant, or you call in or consult professionals to manage or accomplish the work, those strategies and solutions will make your life easier and more enjoyable. Your home and living space will be safer to use.

You will be increasing the level of comfort, convenience, and accessibility in your living environment while reducing the potential for injury, frustration, or unnecessary effort.

You, and the others in your home (and your visitors and houseguests), will have an easier time of seeing, reaching, and using various controls, fixtures, and appliances.

When the changes, solutions, strategies, and methods that have been presented in this text are employed, the immediate result will be the increased enjoyment of your home.

The longer term benefit will be the added value in terms of desirability for future owners.

Resale value should be enhanced because the changes will increase the appeal and broaden the potential purchaser base to a much larger audience.

As much as you look forward to making some, most, or all of the changes to your home that have been presented here (notwithstanding those already done), just think of how much someone else might like to find a home that already has made these changes for them.

Now, It's Up To You

The universal design concepts, treatments, solutions, tips, recommendations, and strategies that I have presented in this book are intended to be used by you to impact and increase the accessibility, safety, comfort, convenience, value (marketability), and visitability of your living space.

Perhaps you can tackle many of these projects yourself. If not, you now know what can be done and how to talk with professionals who can help you achieve the results that you seek.

Now, it's up to you to determine where you want to begin as you start incorporating these features into your home, apartment, or design projects.

You may already have some of these completed. That's a great start, and now you can add to what's already been done.

Begin to prioritize what you want to do, determine which (if any) of the projects you want to do yourself, and then reach out to professionals who can help you with the rest.

Steve Hoffacker

Steve Hoffacker, AICP, CAASH, CAPS, CGA, CGP, CMP, CSP, MCSP, MIRM, is principal of Hoffacker Associates LLC, based in West Palm Beach, Florida. He is a new home sales trainer and sales and marketing coach for remodelers.

Steve is an award-winning new home sales trainer and coach, commercial real estate broker, marketing consultant, award-winning photographer, best-selling author, blogger, teacher, and salesman.

For more than 30 years, he has helped homebuilders, new home salespeople, remodelers, small business owners, and other professional salespeople to be more visible, competitive, profitable, and effective — and to really enjoy themselves as they pursue their business.

He has embraced the concept of universal design and has given you many examples of how to incorporate them into your existing home — as part of normal maintenance and updating or through a larger scale remodeling project.

He interacts with providers from around North America in his classes and has incorporated many of these treatments into his own home so he speaks from practical experience.

Many of the suggestions Steve provides in this book are printed here for the first time. You won't find them anywhere else as of this printing.

the first time

Made in the USA
Lexington, KY
30 August 2015